Edmond's Visionary Path

Edmond's Visionary Path

Past, Present, and Future

Edmond L. Campbell

authorHOUSE®

AuthorHouse™
1663 Liberty Drive
Bloomington, IN 47403
www.authorhouse.com
Phone: 1-800-839-8640

First published by AuthorHouse   10/25/2011

ISBN: 978-1-4634-3608-7 (sc)
ISBN: 978-1-4634-3606-3 (hc)
ISBN: 978-1-4634-3605-6 (ebk)

Library of Congress Control Number: 2011912968

Printed in the United States of America

Any people depicted in stock imagery provided by Thinkstock are models, and such images are being used for illustrative purposes only.
Certain stock imagery © Thinkstock.

This book is printed on acid-free paper.

Contents

Book IV

Book V

Book VI

Book VII

Book X

Preface

I grew up with visions, and I first called them dreams. I have since learned that dreams are defined as involuntary experiences that happen to us during certain stages of sleep. But I do not believe that dreams are just something happening to us. As we focus on and develop the internal building of our mental and spiritual structure, we can better understand our real building blocks. I found my dreams scary sometimes as a child of four or five, but by the time I was six or seven, I found out that they could help me.

In those days—the early fifties—you had to take a nap in the middle of the day until you were a certain age, and I was not yet old enough to go without one. It was summer and warm outside, and I had to take a nap. This would be no ordinary nap and no ordinary day; it would start to define my life in a way that I would never have imagined. I remember seeing my mother dying. I was standing alone, looking at her, and I was crying. I continued to cry until I woke up with my mother's hand on me, comforting me. She told me that I must have had a bad dream. I remember what she said, and I remember the dream still to this day—the mother who woke me was not the mother I was crying over in the vision.

I was six or seven years old and in elementary school when kids started to tease me about being adopted. I never paid any attention to them, and it really did not bother me. The dream I had had was scary to me, but it prepared me for the kids' teasing, because I never forgot the vision; I was not supposed to.

It was also as a child that I met the one I call "OneOther"—who's within me, who walks with me, and who walks for me when I cannot. We first met physically when I was about four or five years old. I was playing marbles with kids outside, and one kid was cheating. His big brother was looking over his shoulder, but I could not let him take my marbles. I grabbed as many as I could and ran for my porch. It was at the end of this run that I first met OneOther. He was within me and simply took over; I moved to the background within me where he normally was. I saw and understood fully what was taking place, and it was seamless: his moving forward and me moving into the background. We both took on the challenge of my defense, which would happen from that point forward throughout the rest of my life—whenever it was necessary and in many different ways.

It was September 9, 1989, when I made my first notation about the marks, lines, and designs I saw on the backside of my hands when I wrote down the visions. I simply made notations of the drawings on my hands, not thinking much of them at that time; it was in 1993 that I started to make full drawings of my hands. The drawings or designs on my hands, arms, and other areas were simply there when I woke up. I did not feel anything or even know they were there, but I noticed them one morning when I started to write down a vision.

It was 2009 when I started to take actual photographs of the markings on my hands as backup to my drawings and the written information.

Edmond Campbell

Introduction

It is important to know how this book works, how the visions with their dates connect to our present time. This book gives you the space to think, but it does not tell you everything to think. The conclusions are yours. I can tell you this: To the best of my ability, I have written exactly what I was given to share with you. Over the years, I have written thousands of visions on most everything and everyone within the larger group concept. It is my personal feeling that this book is an introduction to additional information that I will share with you in the very near future.

Some of the visions in this book do not have dates. In the early years, I wrote them down so I would not forget them but did not add the dates.

Most nights I have from two to three sleep periods, and during one sleep period there can be as many as two to three different visions included; each was given a different letter of the alphabet to separate them.

In this book, you will see what I call marks (///). They were given to me and represent all things from the Father///, the spiritual force of the Father///, and the spiritual essence of the Father///. The Father/// to me is the essence and beginning of all things, not different from the names we use for "the creator" in religions. The spiritual force of the Father/// is what Christianity calls the Holy Spirit///, and the spiritual essence of the Father/// is what I call the Christ Spirit.

Included in this book are drawings of my hands with designs on them. The designs are present about 50 percent of the time when I have visions, and it depends on what the vision is about as to how graphic they are. I do not know at this time how the designs on my hands and body fit with the visions. In time, these visions and hand designs will be revealed. I do know that for thousands of years people have painted and drawn graphic designs on their bodies—long before this modern era. I believe it actually comes from when we did not have to draw them, when they came naturally.

In order to use these visions today, we must add nineteen years starting with 1993, which would make the revealing date 2012. The Mayans use calendars of eleven years and twenty years, but I use a calendar of nineteen years; it was what I was taught. I also use a thirty-day and three-year calendar for all new visions. This should give you an idea of when some of the events will happen, in the hope that you will be able to change or improve the outcome.

Book I

I saw workers running toward a cave with undergrowth in front of it, and they were nearing an area where the children of the *Atlanteans* were playing. The children started to talk to them as they passed by, but the workers did not understand. The children pointed toys at the workers—toy replicates of real weapons—and the workers ran as if the toys were real. They were running for their lives, getting close to the place they had been seeking for safety, a building, the likes of which they had never seen before. It was a rock-type, marble-structured building with a large, round structure attached to its right side. This was where "they" were—they who could help them. The earth trembled as it had for a very long time. It was getting worse each day. The workers finally got close; they were very scared, seemingly of everything. The older Atlanteans did not want them near the buildings and would not let them enter for shelter. Not all of the children born here would be able to return to our home. Some of them would be left behind with elders who would protect and teach them. Everyone else who was able to go was getting ready for the trip—and thinking about those who would be left behind.

We, the Atlanteans, had tried to save our home and the children from the disaster that we had known was coming, but we could not. All was lost, and hope rested in the few elders and children who would be left behind in a cave that had been made for them. We had come here to build a world, before beings of this earth had developed much beyond their days of living in caves. We had specimens made for our work, and we had bought them with us, but as things grew out of hand, some of them got away and were lost to us.

We were the workers of Atlantis. We had dug black metal out of the earth, which sustained the new world being built. But we had grown scared of the noise and scared of the earth shaking under us. One of the

1

buildings sat near a very large hole in the earth; the hole was so large, deep, and wide that I could not see the other side of it, and the earth moved all the time. More black metal was taken, at a great rate, and before long I could not see how deep it was anymore.

We approached the great building, but we were stopped without even a hand being raised at us. Standing in front of us was one of the Young Masters. With only a thought, we were stopped, and we could not move at all.

The Young Master called out, "Guards, take them away," and my name was called.

I was waiting for my time to come, when I would be old enough in spirit to do that—to stop them with only a thought. Soon it would be my time.

There were elders, four who were greater than I was in powers, and they were in a silent place where they could not be disturbed. I felt our time was very short, and all of us who could, had to leave. The workers were trying to overtake us, because they were scared of the earth's vibrations. They knew we would leave, and they would be left behind. This place had become unlivable to us. There had been a long time of destruction, and the area was covered by water.

No Date: Dracula the Vampire Legend and
             What It Really Means to Me

I found myself driving in a car as fast as I could. It was a dark, cloudy night, and I knew that something was following us. I knew it was Dracula. I was afraid, so very afraid that he would catch us. He flew, and I was going as fast as I could to get away from him. I was not ready to face him yet, but there would be a battle someday. With the power of God/// and the "Lost Words," we would have a chance. It was not over yet.

Blessed be the name of the Lord, thy God///, as I recognized meeting the strangest person of this time period—me. By faith and by the power given by God/// to a servant willing to perform the deeds that were given to him, I would somehow defeat and win this one, but the question was, "Would the young lady be saved, and was it who we thought it was?"

Dracula has been around a long time in movies and folklore. He is known by millions on a number of continents, but in this vision, he means something else to me. This vision is telling me about the blood—not external blood and gore, but a bloodline running inside the body, from body to body, carrying a special key to the knowledge of the first visitors. It is also the second vision from the Atlantean vision, which is telling me about the Atlantean bloodline and my destiny with it. What I seem to fear so much in this vision is actually what I am trying to find and understand about myself: the blood that ran through those beings, in what we call Atlantis, runs through me. It is activating now with some of the "old knowledge" of that time to help in our future—a new future that we can change or continue as is. The young lady in this vision comes into view later in visions; I did not see a clear picture of her at this time, it was just the thought "Would the young lady be saved?" that was given to me at this time.

1976 My First Flight and Trying to Fly Alone

It was dark and cloudy as I rose in the air into a flying position. I hit limbs on trees, and I tried to fly higher to get away from them. Finally, I was above the trees, flying free. I decided to turn over on my back, and I just floated along for a while. It felt so good to be able to do that. Then I heard the voice of my father calling me back; that's when I started to get a bad feeling about being up there by myself. I was a little worried about getting back. I felt that if I had continued in the dark, flying alone, something might happen to my physical body.

This vision of my first flight tells me about my path: It might not always be clear where my path will take me, and there will be obstacles along the way. I will obtain levels I would never have expected possible, and I must be properly trained and prepared for them.

1978-1979 I Fell Off a Cliff to the Ground and Walked toward the Light

I found myself walking toward a cliff in the dark, and I could not stop myself. I was going to fall off the edge into the darkness below, but I had no control. I seemed to fall hundreds of feet until I hit the bottom. Lying there on the ground, I did not feel hurt at all, and I had no idea where I was. Why was I not hurt from the fall? I got to my feet slowly because it was total darkness. I looked down, and I could not see my own hands or the ground I was standing on. I stood very still and looked around, trying to see an indication of light coming from some place. There was none. Then, as I stood there, I started to feel something I did not want to feel. It was at that same moment that I saw a light in the distance, which appeared to be a light in a window. I looked at it very hard; it was the shape of a window with light, but I could not see anything else—not a path or even the ground where I would be walking, nothing. For reasons I did not understand, I started to walk toward that light, even though I saw nothing between the light and me. I didn't think I really had a choice.

This vision gives a view of my entire life. Walking to the cliff is my early years as a child on my way to my destiny and a scheduled time and place where the level of my understanding or growth would change. Walking in darkness is simply going through a set portion of my life without a complete picture of my full purpose for being there, moving through it in faith and then knowing. Falling off a cliff is the length of time when I knew something special was happening but did not know what, an age when I could understand things were happening but had no answers. My hitting the bottom would happen in 1992, as the visions increased and my interest in them started to change. It was October 1992, and I was lying on the floor in my living room, looking through a stack of newspapers for the week, when I saw it. It was a story about a murder in Montgomery County, Maryland; a pillowcase had been taken from the house where it happened. I looked back and found a vision I had written only a few days earlier dated October 18, 1992, concerning the murder. What turned the light on for me was a vision on September 19, 1992, where I was looking for a job in an employment office but left without one. Actually, I discovered what part of my future job would be, although these early years would only be to learn and not really get involved; I was behind the information flow, not in front of it.

1984   I See a Giant Tree In Front of Me and a Bright Light to My Right

I found myself walking on beautiful green grass. Everything around me was beautiful, and I walked toward a brightly lit, open area. Walking to my left was a hound dog, and we both saw a giant tree directly in front of us. I stopped and just stood there, looking up into this enormous tree full of green leaves. It was the most beautiful tree I had ever seen. As I continued to look at it, I realized that it was standing in the middle of my path, as if there was no way around it—just this giant tree. To my right was an area that looked like a mist of light radiating from the ground up. I could not tell its height or length, and it was brighter than any day I had ever seen. I noticed the dog walking across the grass, going straight toward the light. As it continued to walk toward the light, I wondered why it did not go for the tree as dogs always do. I watched it walk into the light and disappear. I looked at the tree again and moved closer to it, looking up into it as if something was going to happen.

Finding myself walking simply means that this is my given path, and I must walk it. The beauty all around me means I can and will find beauty and goodness in all things, but as I walk this path, I will see the other side of that beauty and goodness for what it really is. The tree is my Tree of Knowledge of Good and Evil, and it will prepare me for what I will need on the path I must walk. The light to my right is not the light at death, but the light that awaits me after my path is over this time. The hound dog walking to my left was a companion in my early childhood, but I have a companion closer than that to walk with all my life.

1986   Mama Taught Me How to Call on the Father/// for Help

I stood looking down from a mountaintop with my mother. I wanted so much to join all the people I saw below who seemed to be having so much fun near the water. I asked my mother how I could get down to where all the people were so I could have some fun too. We were up so high, and I didn't see any way down from where we were. As I continued to look down, Mama said, "Follow me," and she started to find a way down with me following her. Mama only took a few steps, me right on her heels, when she stopped and turned to face me. She said, as clearly as I have ever heard anything, "Don't call me 'Mama,'" and she walked away. I began to cry; I did not understand why Mama would say that to me. I loved my mother more than anything I knew. I did not care about going down the mountain—I cared about her. I woke from this vision still crying and just sat there on the side of my bed thinking about it. And then it all became so clear to me: "Don't call me Mama," but when you need to call for something, call on the Father///.

This vision tells me about my life of being in the world but not really being part of the world and all that it has become because of our wants and perceived needs. I would be at a vantage point where I could see and understand what the world was doing, and I would have direct knowledge of how we were progressing. In all this, I would need help, and when I did, I would need to call on the Father/// alone and no one else.

03/27/86   10:00 p.m.   My Inner and Outer Beings Becoming One, Part One

I was at North West Street, my home, sitting in the living room on the couch when I felt the need to look out the window behind me. I turned, looking south down West Street, and I saw someone who looked exactly like me coming toward the house. It scared me to see what looked like me running down the sidewalk toward me. I thought that he might want to come in where I was, and I did not want that. I was scared to go out of the house. It was a sunny day and warm, and he was running as if he had everything under control. He was thinner and firmer, with less body weight than I have. He looked like I really wanted to look.

I heard a knock at the door, and I was scared to open it; it could have been him. I thought it was him, but it was some man I had never seen before. He had come to talk about me and the one I saw running down the sidewalk who looked like me. This man told me I should try to see myself face-to-face—why, I did not know. At this point, my stepson walked in, and the man and I began to talk to him about all this and what I felt. Both of them finally left, and I decided I would definitely not look out of that again window.

Then I was the one running down the sidewalk toward the house with one thing on my mind: to go up to the window to scare the one in the house. At that point, I woke up.

3/28/86   2:30 a.m.   My Inner and Outer Beings Becoming One, Part Two

[This was continuing the same vision above in 10:00 p.m., but here I called myself "B" and he was "A," the one who stayed in the house.]

This time, I was walking along a path with two men—one black, one white—and both were unshaven and dirty, as if they were drunk. As we walked, they told me about myself as "B" and about when I would join "A" as one. We walked to the side of an old, run-down shed, and just as one of the men was about to sit down in what looked like an outdoor bathroom, he was warned not to because something unsightly was on the surface of the wood.

We started to walk again, and they continued to talk to me about what was going to happen. We reached a place where two German shepherd dogs on heavy chains jumped out at us. We walked around the first one, but as we approached the second dog and started to pass it, the men with me seemed afraid. For some reason I was not afraid, and I walked between the two dogs and knelt down, staring at them. I called them to come to me, and one at a time, they came and sat down by me. Because of this, I thought, Why can't I be one with A now? So I asked the two men, but they said it was not the right time yet. They said the time would come soon. I felt powerful and strong in mind—able to do things that I had only thought about doing before. We continued. I thought about how I felt; I had never felt anything like it before. Then we stopped at a place where I was given three envelopes containing something very important, but for some reason I insisted it should be four, and that there was one more envelope I was supposed to have. They would not give me a fourth envelope, so I kept the three they did give me and walked on down the path. These alphabet letters were given to me just before I woke up: E O T A.

The letters "E O T A" came with no understanding of their meaning at this time. Both the 10:30 p.m. and 2:30 a.m. visions tell me about two extreme individual strengths becoming one. In my life so far, it has always been one or the other at a time, with knowledge of both at the same time. I first became aware of the force within me at the early age of about four or five years old, and I did not realize what was happening but just lived with it. It was only in emergency or threatening situations that it would take over, and I would simply look on from the background. At the time of this vision, I had experienced it many times over the years—being physically both at the same time.

12/ 22/86   Jesus, Mother Mary, and a Female Child Together

I was afraid. I was running away from a woman who was dressed completely in black and who chased me with something in her hand that looked like an ice pick. She was gaining ground on me, so I entered a building to get away from her. As I passed a door on my right, I saw three people, and I recognized one of their faces as Jesus. I stopped, turned around, and went back to the room. As I went through the door, I saw two females in the room and the back of Jesus as he was walking toward another door leaving the room. The two females were standing as he left, and as I looked at them, I could see one of them was Mother Mary. There was a young girl very close to her whom I did not know. She turned to me as I asked her for help, and the three of us left the room. We went into a larger open area where there were chairs; she sat down, and the young woman sat down beside her. She asked me to sit down, but I was too scared to sit. All I could think of was trying to find a way to stop the woman in black from hurting me. I asked Mother Mary when would Jesus be returning, and she said soon, but I was just too scared to wait with that woman after me.

I woke up from this vision mad at myself. I should have believed her at once and sat down beside her and just waited as she asked.

Book II

I got in bed and meditated on nothing for a while, and then all of a sudden I was listening to an elder talk to me about my impatience. I knew without a doubt that he was right, and I started to hear him very clearly. He told me to look at the water, and I noticed I was now sitting by the river near my home. He said, "See how fast it is running? Now slow it down until it almost stops, and then touch the water." I did as he asked. I do not know how long it took, but I began to breathe deeper until I came out of it. I turned over in my bed and looked at the mirror. I saw a reflection from the window, and then I was in another room. This room had what looked like tests on its walls, and there were bells that I had to ring, and I made them all ring. I felt a pressure inside me like being high up in an airplane. I turned around, and there was a table with two chairs. On the wall behind the table were religious pictures of different types. I noticed a box of crayons and some glasses with beer or alcohol in them on the table. Then, right before my eyes, it all became clearer, and the crayons were still on the table, but the glasses were gone. Slowly it all faded, but I knew exactly what it meant to me. I got up, went to the mirror, and checked my face, and where I normally had one line I had three on my forehead.

One of the elders from my original Atlantis experience came to guide me on how to meditate, but the important thing was my preparation for the work I must be able to do. The religious items on the wall were from many different religions. The beer or alcohol needs to be left behind as I go forward. The two chairs at the table represent the one who will guide me in all of this and myself, as the Father/// decides.

08/19/89   3:30 a.m.   Atlantis Continues with the Preparation
                           of a Cave

For the first time, we were being trained concerning a possible cave-in, and we were told what to expect and how we should react in case it happened in our new home. We were guided into a great underground dwelling, larger than a football field; it would become our new home for as long as we had to stay. In the middle of this giant cave was a lake of water that we walked around. We moved into the cave all types of things to keep us alive for a long time. We sealed the openings of the cave with lasers to keep out the upper world; it would be our only chance to survive. Some of our kind had to stay outside because this cave could only keep a certain number of us alive for the required length of time. I had a daughter. We all had mates and made love in what we called "The Great Room" in our new home. It was our home now. Digging, you could find the three other elders.

A time shall come when this great underground cave will be found, and the graves of our earliest visitors will be there untouched.

Book III

06/07/91   3:25 a.m.   Bill Clinton as a Young Boy Playing
Baseball

I sat in the stands at a baseball game, watching little kids play baseball. As I sat there, I saw a little boy playing the outfield for the first time. When the ball came to him, it fell short. He put his glove down to catch it, but it rolled away from him and then rolled back. The ball was doing odd things whenever it was around him.

I asked a little boy near me who that young boy was, and he said, "Bill." To me, Bill looked to be about eight years old. I went close to him, but it was not the right time, so I waited.

04/07/92   4:45 a.m.   Two Past-Life Experiences and the
Atlantis Disaster

I found myself standing in line with many other men, waiting for some reason, when I saw the military driving up in different types of vehicles. It made me think. I had always wanted to be an officer in the army. The next thing I knew, I was on a military bus headed somewhere with the army.

(a) A white sergeant first class met me on Sunday when I arrived and took me to a house where a black staff sergeant lived. I was going to stay there for a while. He welcomed me in, but almost immediately, I felt the need to use the bathroom. I followed him to it, and he pointed at the door. I went inside. I saw the toilet, but I had no idea how to use it or what to do; I must have forgotten how to use one. It was then that I looked in the mirror. I saw my uniform: it was airborne infantry, and I was a captain. It seemed as if it was the first time I saw my face. I had always wanted to be a captain in the army, but my face was another black man's face. As I opened my mouth, my bottom teeth were mostly missing. I saw that a lot of work had been done to my mouth to repair the extensive damage received when I was in a prisoner-of-war camp in Vietnam in the 1960s. As I looked around the bathroom, I saw the fixture I was supposed to sit on, but I had forgotten how to use it—I was used to squatting down. My name was Captain C. Crisp, US Army.

(b) I went back further: I was black with lots of white hair, and my skin was very black, like armor for protection. We were very smart and educated. I had never seen a white species of any kind. It was 30,000 BC, and I found I could travel back thousands of years without losing who I really was as I looked through the eyes of others.

    (a) Somewhere, I was not sure exactly where it happened, my body was badly hurt. My legs were full of pain, and the pain in one of my legs was much worse than the other. I was in a southern town. I was a member of the Eighty-Second Airborne Division, and I was wounded very badly.

    (b) I was a black man from long ago, when the knowledge base was being destroyed because we had taken it too far and advanced our understanding far beyond what we could control. We had worked among the new humans as if we were gods. Some of us forewarned our people that a disaster was eminent. Some paid little attention, while others were saved. The knowledge and information we developed was lost to us at our own choosing, as we had grown too old of mind and too powerful. Some of us agreed that something had to be done. We decided the world as it was would be better off without the knowledge at that time. We had gotten to the point that there was no sickness and no death—we passed on when we wanted to. We did not want others to find it, not even our children, but it could still be claimed, and some of the information was given to other groups to learn and carry forth.

Some of the untold history was about the laws we had set for everyone and how we ourselves broke some of them in our curiosity to learn everything. When the end came, some of us lived on to teach others. We did not judge what their future actions might be. The true knowledge would be known once again. Some of us did as we were taught by the elders, but others did not. They would not share the knowledge as we were supposed to.

Children were born only to those who did good works, and the women taught them the knowledge and guided the family group. The knowledge grew too great for us to handle; women did nothing wrong, but we ourselves did—we went too far and thought too much about the accomplishments we had acquired.

Dark skin and hair afforded us the best protection from the new world. The oxygen content was different then, and we took in much more oxygen for dissemination. We were the closest to our creator, yet we never saw him, and no one had.

[In this vision, I move back and forth between the earliest beings of earth and the staff sergeant, and I use the alphabet to separate the different periods as the vision was given to me.] Even in this life today, I have pain in my legs and more pain in one than the other. It has continued to follow me. I have been in the military too, only three years this time, but I have always felt that I knew a lot more about military strategy than three years would have had the opportunity to teach me.

It is here that the Adam and Eve story started: the knowledge was too great, yet the inner spirit had its beginning, its roots of knowledge still in our children, and we simply did not teach them as we once did. It meant that that the children were cut off and left to grow and develop without the old knowledge that was usually passed down one to another.

04/07/92   Adam and Eve Were the Second Chance, Not the First

Adam and Eve of the Bible were the second chance for humans, not the first. We walked with them, taught them, and they grew without us. They live to this day by our knowledge. We had a plant that grew like a tree. It extended life, and we would take this plant and live with excellent health for hundreds of years until we grew tired. We would then stop and pass on. We knew not to fear death, and understood that death is the regenerator of life—that the spirit regenerates, obtaining additional wisdom along the way as it gives to the individual bodies along the path. We must learn to share and to help each other in everything we do, and only then can we see what is before our eyes, the creation. The Creator/// is not a women or man, figuratively speaking. Israel got man from Adam and Eve, who we taught to live and start again. The Tree of Knowledge of Good and Evil was simply us not teaching our young children the old knowledge because we were afraid for them, afraid of what it did to us. Some bits and pieces of the old knowledge they have but not the root.

04/07/92   The Second Coming of the One with Knowledge

The second coming would be the old knowledge renewed in someone of this time, and the warning of the Antichrist is simply to stop the belief in the one with the old knowledge. The Antichrist, no, information and knowledge to share, yes. It has been known from old teachings and books from long ago that the one with the old knowledge would return. This was never shared down through our present history, but the knowledge is known by some in this day, and they hoard it, keeping it away from the people.

Jesus partook of this knowledge and believed completely and was rewarded for his life's work, not in faith but in knowing, a step above faith. Shall Jesus return, we all return, for we are not finished yet. But the return of the one called the Christ is different. Jesus was said to have had the spark of Christ///, the anointing, and at that time the use of the knowledge had to be stopped because they thought he would reveal all in time.

Book IV

09/19/92   Interview for a Job in Thirty Days

I went to an employment agency looking for a job, and as I walked in I saw a man being interviewed. The interviewer stopped and asked me what I wanted and stated I must be in the wrong place, but I sat down by an admiral who was also looking for a new job. I thought about the words said to me—it felt like racism. I told them so, as the one who said it was then interviewing the admiral. There were three interviewers total, and the other two were better than the first man. My new job started thirty days from then, on October 18, 1992.

My written history in the pages before this leads me to my future path or direction. I call it my appointed task, part of what I am to do this time around. It would be a little over thirty days from this day that I would notice an article in the Washington Post about a murder that happened in Montgomery County, Maryland. It opened my eyes, and I contacted the police department in Montgomery County and went out to their offices. There they copied sections of my book, and I later faxed them additional information that I thought might be useful. It was later that I realized that the second part of the vision was also connected, and it was where bodies were buried. I would go on to find many other newspaper articles, and they too would only be thirty days from the previous date.

I also realized, months later, that receiving these visions was not for me to share now, that it could not close a case; it was not direct enough to be helpful. But I finally figured out when I would be able to use it: 2011-2013, nineteen years in the future to be more precise. It was the Mayan calendar. In 2009 I found out I could use the eleven-year Mayan calendar and my nineteen-year calendar with my visions; in the past I used only the three-year and thirty-day calendars.

10/18/92   Murder of a Young Woman in Montgomery County, Maryland

(a) I saw myself pushing a lawnmower, cutting grass. A friend I knew tried to sell me another one that I did not need. I had been in the house earlier, and now I saw others go there to help. A Spanish person lived there, and she let me come in when I told her what work I had come to the house to do. There was another younger woman there, maybe in her twenties or thirties; I saw myself walk away from the house with a pillowcase in my hands.

(b) People Buried in the Ground

I passed three dead bodies laying next to cut-up vegetables and other food ready for cooking, and it was all on the same blanket in the same area. I was riding a black horse—just he and I going home. When I reached the clearing where I lived, an old man welcomed me back home. There were horses and cows all painted black in tar; two smaller horses painted in tar were inside a cage. I left a woman there, and I heard someone say, "She might tell who did this," as I rode away.

This was the first time I saw a news article (from the Washington Post during October of 1992) connected with a vision I had. I actually did not know what to do with it or about it. I knew I had information concerning the murder, but I did not clearly understand it myself. The pillowcase drew my attention to it. In part b, I knew the body was where he lived and ate, but I did not know he had training as a chef. I did inform the Montgomery County police, and I went to their office in Rockville, Maryland. The painting of the animals with tar represents possible mutilation or death of animals earlier, before human life started to be taken.

10/24/92   A Carful of Presidents except Two

We were in a car, going west toward the mountains in Virginia, the president of the United States and me. First, I was driving him, and then he drove me. He was not one of today's candidates; he was someone I did not know, but he was president. He took over driving, and I rode in the back seat. At times, he was driving so fast that I thought the state troopers were going to stop us. We passed three cars full of state police, and the last one waved at us. A few miles up the road, our car was full of men, including another black man who was driving. That was when we were stopped by security. The security team asked for me and said that Mark Albright told them to talk to me, but I did not know a Mark Albright; I did know a Madeleine Albright.

Coming from the east, going west, was a future event, but it is now. I was driving the president, who I say represents Barack Obama, our president. Driving him first is his first four years in office, and when he is driving me is the second four years of his term when I would come into view. Mark Albright is actually Madeleine Albright, Secretary of State then, who represents our present Secretary of State now. That could change.

11/10/92   3:48 a.m.   Three Tornadoes Side by Side Coming Our Way

I was in Gum Springs, Virginia, on the way to our house with my dad. Dad's watermelon crop was spread out everywhere and caught my eye. Mama was in the house; it was an old wooden house but still in good shape. I was looking out the window when I saw tornados—three of them, side by side, coming our way. They were white and full of water. Dad started to talk to me as we looked at them; they were six feet apart and very dangerous. When they hit the house, it was so fast I could hardly believe what was happening. It knocked down everything except our house, but then a tree fell down on it. It broke a small window, but the water did not come in. Mama and I lay on the floor and waited until it was over. When we went outside to see our melon crop, it did not look any different—nothing had happened to it at all.

In this vision, I saw three tornadoes, side by side, coming from the west going east, and when this did happen a few days later, it was actually over a three-day period of time: November 21-23, 1992. It was called a tornado outbreak, and it ended up in our backyard.

12/22/92   4:15 a.m.   Lifted by the Back of My Neck and Taken on a Trip

I was in my room, and all of a sudden, I was grabbed by the back of my neck, raised up, and taken out of my room without going through anything. I was shown many things: restaurants, hotels, and buildings of all kinds. I ended up at the house of a friend of mine, Simon. We were in the yard with many people, and I rubbed shoulders with them. Simon was a friend of the family. I went everywhere Simon did, always up off the ground but not out of reach, and I talked to him. I told him I must be there because of him, and he looked at me and said no. I was then taken back the exact same way, seeing all the beautiful lights along the way until I reached my apartment. I was still being held by the back of my neck up in the air. As I was held there, I saw my apartment. It was full of spiders, bugs, and all types of things I did not see before. I wondered why I had not seen them. I was taken to all four corners of my bedroom, with my face pressed up against the wall, and I started to wonder exactly what was happening to me. I began to think of Jesus///, and I prayed. I was placed down on the floor in the southeast corner of my room, and I prayed with my face touching cobwebs in the corner. I was again lifted by the back of my neck and put in a chair where my hair was cut. My eyes closed, but I opened them just a little and saw the shadow on the wall of that which was taking care of me; I had no idea what it was. I closed my eyes again, and it began to fix my eyes. I slowly woke up.

Lifted by the back of my neck from my room, taken to see all that the world has to offer, and then taken to Simon's house is very specific and direct. This vision tells me I will have the chance to see many things, but I have a job to perform—a mission in the future that is unknown to me at this time. Returning home, my eyes were opened to things at a minor level, and being taken around my room with my face up against the wall at the ceiling level tells me something else. I will be given all four corners of this place at some point, but first I must understand where my strength comes from, directly from the Father///. It was in 2010 when I actually started to pray in the southeast corner. A vision I had was like being talked to, and at the end of it, my covers were lifted, and I was actually dumped out of bed into that corner, where I prayed for some time. When I woke up from this vision, I did get up and say a very short prayer that went like this: "Thank you, Father/// for all things. Thank you for this wonderful day and for my brothers and sisters all over the world wherever they may be." I knew that this was the time to change my manner of praying. The preparation of my hair and eyes is not a physical thing but means inner preparations will begin to take place.

Book V

01/01/93   4:21 a.m.   A Big Black Bird Enters My Bedroom Window

I heard something at the window; I looked, and it was a big black bird. It came in my bedroom window and passed me, and it went out into the other rooms where all the people were. I began to hear the people calling out for help, calling me to get the birds out. As I opened the door, many birds passed me going back into my bedroom. They were all sizes, all colors and shapes, and someone said they were souls. I was supposed to be guarding the way, but I was a little afraid of that big black bird. I got them all back in the bedroom and closed the door, but I did not know how long I could hold them, because I could not seal it. I did not know how long I could hold them in because there were so many of them.

This is the beginning of the 2012 countdown for this book using the Mayan calendar, using the twenty-year span starting from the date of this vision. I have always used nineteen years, but what I read and saw said twenty years.

01/03/93   8:46 a.m.   On My Finger Was a Wedding Band First
                         and Then the Star of David

I had a room, but someone had changed the furniture around in it. I later went outside and got lost. I could not find my way back to the room, and so I wandered over to Washington Street and stood by the bus stop. I was standing there because two men had been following me, and I was scared they would hurt me. I did not have anything, and I had no money to ride the bus. At the bus stop, a man was giving away chances to win something, but you had to sign something to take the chance. I asked him if he had number 263, and he said, "Wait a minute." He didn't know exactly what numbers he had. My clothes were very bad, and I looked bad.

19

I was a street person, but I lived with someone else. They had changed the furniture around, and now I could not find my way back.

The man giving away chances asked me if I graduated and asked where my class ring was. I said, "I don't know," but as I lifted my hand up, two rings were on it, and one of them I knew: a gold ring with a single star with different colors; it was the Star of David. The other ring was a plain wedding band. Both rings were on the same finger, the wedding band was first and then the Star of David.

01/20/93   2:38 p.m.   My Age Is the Chapters in the Book of Isaiah

We sat around the table, three of us, and I looked into their faces; one was a face of a black-skinned man, who I first saw smiling but who now had turned to tears. I put my hand on his knee and said, "I will help you."

Also at the table was a young boy who was sitting to my right. We talked, and I told him about the things I wanted to do. I touched his hand, but it was not there. I asked him if he believed we could do it—change things—and he said, "Maybe we can." Then he said, "Remember Isaiah and the women." I asked him what he thought, and again he said, "Maybe we can," fading in and out, first as flesh and then spirit, back and forth, as I looked at him.

The first man, who had had a smile on his face that had turned to tears, now had blisters where the tears had been, and he seemed to have lost all hope. On my left, the man looked to be eighteen to twenty years old, and on my right, the boy looked to be ten to twelve years old, with a baby face that I remembered as only being five or six years old. I had touched both men; the one on my left, his face changed from a smile to tears and then blisters, and on my right, the boy faded in and out, first flesh and then spirit.

Both these beings are one, and that one is me, and my strength lies in both of them and in my Father/// who strengthens and guides me. From a young boy to an older man, I will finish my walk on this path, but it will not be easy.

3:46 p.m.   I Stand in an Empty Auditorium Wearing a Suit and Tie

I was a little boy four or five years old, wearing a suit and tie and talking from a stage in a large room, but no one was there except me.

As an older man in my later years, I may have the opportunity to talk to many people in many places.

02/24/93   2:11 p.m.   Carried by My Feet Upside Down

A man dressed like the men of biblical days carried me by my feet, upside down, into a room that had no windows or doors and laid me down on my face in a straightway position. He touched the back of my head while saying some words I could not understand, and he tapped me three times on the back of my head and told me to rise to a kneeling position. I prayed. Permission was given to me, and I rose to my feet. He talked to me. He sat in a large, squared chair with arms, and his robe draped all the sides of the chair. He had long hair with a beard, and his skin was brown. I cried and held my hands out to him. I was scared and afraid to approach him without his approval. He held my two hands and said I would be okay, and I turned and went through seven white walls.

People were in all of the areas I passed through, as if between the seven walls there were seven houses or periods of time that I had to pass through. The last wall I passed through placed me in the back of a store that sold exercise equipment. The first thing I noticed was two round balls, like the weights that shot-putters use, a black one and a gray one. Behind me walked a man with a suit on, a white man, and he smelled me from behind. I looked at myself; I had old clothes on, and maybe I did smell a bit. I did not have any money to buy anything, so they called the police on me, and as I started to walk out of the store, the one who smelled me, grabbed me. I turned around and grabbed him by both of his arms, and as I held him, I began to talk to him. He started to cry as the police arrived, but they just looked on as I continued to talk to him.

2:11 p.m.   Left and Right Hand Backside

21

03/09/93 2:46 a.m. Germans Held Jewish People in Cages, I Was in a Cage

We walked around in cage-type jails, underground, with bars on all sides except for the back wall. German soldiers with guard dogs were left outside our cells most of the time. I was near others but was separated when they put a little girl seven or eight years old in the cage with me. She constantly bothered me to help her. The little girl would cry, because she thought I did not care about what was going to happen to her; I did care, but I was not going to do what they wanted me to. The little girl was afraid they would come for her and wanted me to help her before they came. I just could not do it, I could not commit that. I felt they wanted me to commit a crime against my own laws, a crime that God///would never forgive.

The guards with dogs came into the cell area. They mostly looked at her and only glanced at me on the way out. My cell was a step up off the ground while the larger cells were on the dirt floor—cages like jails, filled with grown-ups and children. I did not see many people, but I could see the guard coming a long way off because there were no walls. We were dressed in white open-type gowns and everyone dressed the same. I felt they used or operated on us for some reason.

4:55 a.m. Picked Up by the Back of My Neck Again

I was on an old military-green bus—headed home I thought. George was the driver, and as he got to my turn, he could not make the turn for some reason. He started to turn another way, and I hollered at him: "Stop, let the bus go where it wants to go." Others on the bus were scared of his driving too. The bus took us to a high-priced housing and business area and stopped. I walked to the front of the bus and got off; he turned the bus around fast and left me. I was mad, but I understood they were scared. As I stood there, it started to happen to me.

I was picked up off my feet by the back of my neck and rammed into the sharp-edged corner of an old, ugly, wood house. As my body went through the walls, I felt everything. I was so scared. I felt my body being pushed through the splintered wood. My lips, my body, all hurt so badly, but I could do nothing. When it was finished, I was dropped in the front yard where it had picked me up. I was in pain, hurting, and I could not get up. I could not do anything except lie on my side, hoping someone would help me. I heard a dog in the distance, and that scared me too, because I could not do anything to help myself. If it came this way, I could not fight it off. I just lay there, feeling broken and in pain, and no one came to help me. My face and lips had been slammed into the sharp corner of the house, I had seen the nails in the wood, and I had felt all of it.

The above vision concerns my physical life in the near future. I will have financial opportunities but at a great cost. Learning both physically and spiritually will not be an easy path to follow; some of the people I meet may not be as helpful as they could be. I must learn that the path I am on is one I will have to face mostly alone, and each day I will have to face what comes. It is a lonely path that not many will understand, and I should not look for much external help.

03/18/93   3:46 a.m.   Houses Built on the Sides of Mountains and Up in Trees

(a) I was riding out the back road on my bicycle, going to pay my rent in Gum Springs. I was sure of where I was supposed to go until I got about halfway there, and then I was not sure anymore. When I saw where I needed to go, I walked into a fenced area and went over to the gate, but it was locked. I turned around to leave, but someone had locked the gate behind me. I started to go under the locked fenced area, and I thought I could make it, but that would be breaking their rules, and so I turned around, my bicycle in hand. That's when I saw a new door and went through it. The land and the picture of how everything looked were so very clear, but I had no idea at all where I was or if I could get back home. As I looked around, I saw a bag full of maps just lying there. I then saw a man and asked him where I was, and he said, "In Niger," like Niger in Africa.

(b) My father and I were in my car driving some place, laughing and talking with each other along the way, when we found ourselves in the state of Maryland. We started seeing houses being built on the sides of a mountain. I first saw this when they were lowering one house down to sit on the side of the mountain. I could not believe it; how could a house stay on the side of a mountain like that? It looked as if it would fall off. I thought of a joke to tell Dad. I told him, "If a man woke up drunk, he could walk out of his front door and fall all the way down here where we are; that's a long way from the top." Dad then called me to come to the other side of the road where he was. He positioned me to lean a certain way so I could see better, and he pointed to the other side of the mountain. I looked, and I saw houses finished and painted, and I knew they had to be cheaper than the others we saw at first.

(c) Before the houses on the mountain, we saw tree houses of a certain size and shape, very high up in the trees. The trees looked to have grown thousands of feet into the air. I would never get there in the first place if I had to climb, and some of them had no side walls, just floors, and no railings to hold on to. Some of the tree houses were completed, just as some of the houses were completed on the side of the mountain. The last thing I saw was where the tree houses were. There were no houses on the ground at all, and I wondered where they were and why.

03/30/93   Right hand, back side

05/04/93   1:05 a.m.   I Am in a South American Indian Village
                         Up in the Mountains

I was in one of the villages in the mountains, and as I walked through the streets alone, I saw kids everywhere looking at me; they always wanted me to give them something. I heard one small child crying, and the sound was coming from under a coat lying in the street. Someone was under it, and it sounded like a girl. I reached down and removed the coat to get her up. I told her there was shelter everywhere. She said that she could not find shelter, and so I took her by the hand to find some. As we started for shelter, a boy cried out, "She is my sister." Then I saw a woman, who probably was the mother, hollering at me to let her go. I let her hand go, and she went back to them. As I walked to the edge of the town, it all became small behind me. Over the hills and into the valley I ran—fast, as something bothered me. I looked back and saw that something was following me; the people did not follow me but something else did.

I then took to the air, and I saw telephone poles and electric lines. I climbed higher all the time. Whatever was behind me also flew. Whatever it was had me scared, so scared I wanted to wake up, and I did. [When I get too scared, I can wake myself up—it is my recourse, my way out.]

When I first went into the little town, I was dressed in a hat and long coat, and I saw all the people and found that they were all shorter than me. I did not know who I was, but the children were not afraid of me. The grown-ups stayed away and just stared. They did not want to be near me. It rained all the time, mostly at night for some reason.

05/17/93   3:26 a.m.   My First Vision with "OneOther"

We were down in the country at my grandfather's place, the place with white grass, but it was different in that the land was opposite of ours—a square piece of land with a road around it. We were on the land, and I knew it was there. At first, it was okay; it did playful things as a child would, and it seemed to be all right. Then it became different, why I am not sure, but it started to do spiteful things. If I wanted something, it would not let me have it. It did not hear or know what I was thinking, but my actions were always challenged. I had picked up a phone and put it down, and then it picked up the same phone and put it down. Then it picked up the phone again and held it over my head and threw it in one corner and broke it. And when I was standing in the field with a garden tool and set it down, it picked it up and threw it over the fence out of my reach. It started to do all kinds of things like that.

Then a fire started, or it started the fire, in a tree. I drove close to it and wanted to put it out, but I was too scared to get out of the car. I stayed inside the track or square of land, and I did not go outside of it. It would throw things inside the track or four corners where I was. I also prayed, and as I did, it got worse, like when it took the telephone above my head, but I did not stop.

I am often shown a picture of some facts that would otherwise be hard to wrap my normal thinking process around—like when you are a little boy scared to death to face the bully, and then you take the chance. At four or five years of age I had no idea what the power or source of this was, but we were one; I never asked or called, it just acted when needed.

In this vision, I am shown and given a picture of the one I now call "OneOther." I am shown how it interacts with me, how it gets things seemingly out of my reach back within my grasp. The reality is it magnifies what I do and even makes what I think possible, but only when necessary or I am not able to do it. It also knows the right way I should do things, and when I am wrong, I suffer for it to some extent. I have to live within my given parameters of right and wrong, which is the Ten Commandments for me, no matter what someone else does.

Book VI

06/27/93   Left and Right Hand, Backside

07/02/93   6:03 a.m.   Mind-Control Testing

On my first IQ test I scored 177, but I cheated, because I knew every question and knew the answers they wanted, as I simply read their minds. I was with a general as an aide. I did not tell him his business, but I simply told him my feelings on different matters. The general had only two stars, a major general. There were three others with us, and they began to talk to me about different things. One of them asked me a question about my test score, and for a minute, I did not know what he was talking about. Then I understood, and I told him it was 177. He looked at his partner, talking in sign language, and I thought to myself, I have never taken a test, and I would never have taken one unless my father wanted me to.

The general went inside a large meeting room with two guys, one white and one black, one in uniform and one in a striped athletic suit, which was black, yellow, and purple. When the general went in, he wished everyone good luck. Sitting in the room, I felt right away that one guy there was going to be a problem. I could feel how strong in mind he was, and it was directed at me. He was attempting to play his game with me, and it made me mad; I ended up not using my gift as I should have, and I began to play with him. I put it into his head he was a child crying, but he caught on to me right away. We continued to do a couple of things back and forth, until he just laughed—that's when it came to me to calm down my thoughts quickly. Why is he so mean, I thought. He should cry like a

27

baby. When I thought that, it started immediately, and he went down on his knees, crying. I stopped, and he went away.

09/18/93   6:33 a.m.   There Is a Right Way Out of the Economic Problem

I was headed to Spring Bank, to the Quander Road area where I used to live. I was trying to find my car that a friend had borrowed, and on the way, I got two apples off of a tree. I did not see my car in the area where I lived, so I walked toward Beacon Hill Road on a concrete walkway. That's when I saw kids and parents together as if they were on a hiking trip. I walked to one side of the walkway as close as I could because of what I was carrying. The walkway was below ground, and once in it, you had to walk until the end of it. I saw that at the end there was a concrete wall or barrier and no way to get out; you had to climb out. As I got closer, I saw other people just waiting. There were two men who I found out worked for the government, the family that seemed to be on a hiking trip, and me—all trying to get out from inside this round concrete wall. We were surrounded by the wall, and it was a bit too high for me to get over. I kept trying, but I wasn't making any headway. The two government men said we could not climb over the five-foot broken concrete wall that surrounded us, and I started to feel they did not want us to get out and continue on our way.

I finally had found something to stand on. I had steel rods and put them up onto the land area outside of the hole with a couple of cans of tuna fish I also had. We were talking about getting out, and that's when one of the kids picked up my paint thinner and dropped it. It went everywhere, and as I turned to look back at him, I saw a way to walk around the wall and get out of there instead of climbing out. It was there all the time, but none of us had seen it.

The whole time I just kept thinking about how I was dressed and that they were all looking at me because my clothes were not clean as they could be.

The concrete walkway is fixed, and the round barrier that is cracked or broken just seems to be impenetrable. The collection of people are random, as is our society, and the government men represent the part of the reason and advice we have gotten about why we cannot get out of the trouble we are in. The steel rods were about four feet long, and are building blocks for the future, the tuna fish represents a time when we will need to work with less, but we still live. The paint thinner is a way of spreading out our problem over time. The boy or young man is the key to spreading the problem out wisely.

8:29 a.m.   A Vision like Daniel of the Bible—Three Black Cats and the Economy

(a) I was walking down Quander Road going southeast, near where I lived. I was headed toward a concrete barrier at Beacon Hill Road. It was then that I noticed three black cats following me on my right side. I saw three adult cats, and I waved my right hand across their backs and two of them changed, and there were two baby kittens and one large cat that had not changed. As I walked down the road a few feet more toward the concrete barrier, they continued to walk to my right. I again waved my right hand across their backs, and they changed to the size and thickness of pencils. They were still walking but were very thin. When I got closer to the round concrete barrier, two of the cats were small kittens again, and one wore a diamond bracelet around its neck. The other small kitten had a gold watch around its neck, and it stood on the back of the one with the diamond bracelet. The other large thin cat was gone, and I did not see at all. It was a bright shining day, and I began to run away from the cats, going up Beacon Hill Road.

The three large cats show the prosperity we felt we had, but no one thought about telling us about cost and that we were using our prosperity too fast.

The two baby cats mean our prosperity would be drained by two-thirds over a period of time, and the one large cat would give us a false sense of our wealth.

Then all three cats change to the size and thickness of pencils, still walking, but very slow. Our wealth would be gone, and the needs would be made up with the pencil—use the pencil and make all the money you need for the budget.

Then changes are made, and two thin cats become regular baby cats again; but the one large thin cat is gone—only two cats remain. The baby cats show the start of rebuilding our wealth, but we must be aware of the future. One of the kittens now wears a diamond bracelet and the other a gold watch, and the one with the watch stands on the back of the one with the diamond bracelet.

There is a time period that will end for building the wealth on the backs of our children and raising them to only think of building wealth; those ways will end.

If proper changes are made, and everyone looks toward a new future with change and advancement, you can keep what you make. If you think because things have changed you will stay the old course, your time will run out.

The concrete barrier means these things will happen for certain. The waving of my right hand means you have control of all of this, and it is now present and will be as I said, unless you change. Getting your house in order must help everyone in some way as you go forward.

Told to Look for a Special Black Snake

(b) I was still on Quander Road, close to where I used to live on Quander Road, and I was looking for a special black snake. I was told exactly where to find it. I needed to capture it in a wooden box. I had what I needed to do it, and as I approached the field where they were supposed to be, I saw an empty field full of snakes. As I looked over the entire field, I saw rattlesnakes, cobras, and every other kind of snake writhing all over each other in a large mass, but I was looking for only one. With a long stick in my right hand, I walked to the edge of the field and put down my box. I started to move through the snakes, looking for the one black one, but they were moving too fast, all over each other. As I moved among them, pushing and pulling them, none of them tried to strike. Then I found the black snake I was after. I grabbed it, took it to the edge of the field, and put it in the box. I turned back to the field, and all the snakes were gone. I turned back to the box near the road, and it was gone too. As I looked over my shoulder at the field again, it looked as if buildings had been on it at one time but were now torn down. Now all that was left was just enough to see that there was once something there in that space. It was just an empty field between two houses, with a small hill of dirt and no grass, weeds, or anything at all. I turned to looked back where the wood box lay at the edge of the field near the road, and there was an oily spot on the ground where it was, nothing else.

To me, this means I have a job to perform, and I will have the necessary tools to get it done. I have a direction and path, and I understand there will be many things along the way, but if I stay true to my path, all will be fine, and the final result will not be mine but the Father's/// to decide.

09/20/93   A Potato-like Object Is an Asteroid

I saw a man worrying about an object or a piece of equipment he could not stop, and it looked like a potato but with needlepoint coming out of it. I called this person an angel, because he was so worried, it was reflected in his mind—only this and the condition of the object were on his mind—nothing else at all.

My Potato-Looking Asteroid

On March 24, 1994, the Washington Post *reported on an asteroid that was near earth. I had this vision about six months before the report.*

09/25/93   9:17 a.m.   Acts, the Twenty-Ninth Chapter of the Bible

I told the group that a large portion belongs to Acts, the twenty-ninth chapter of the Bible, and they divided what was before them accordingly.

Book VII

04/10/94   3:30 a.m.   John the Baptist and His Followers

I was a member of John's group. He was the head and many others followed him, but most members of the group did not like me. It was because it seemed that the rules of the group did not apply to me. One day I found out that there were clothes being given away very close to where we were. Many people rushed to get them, and I decided to see what I could find. I left the meeting, going out the narrow door opening to where the clothes were being given away. When I got there, I found nothing for myself, but I did find John an overcoat, extra-large, and I took it to him. I walked into the meeting area with the coat and sat down to wait until John came to that part of the room so I could give it to him. I gave it to him, and he really liked it, but the others did not. They were trying to get him to be against me.

4:04 a.m.   John the Baptist and the Cross

John was to change the words inscribed on the bottom of the cross as it stood there, and he was to start his work right away.

05/26/94   6:49 a.m.   Children in a Cave—the Atlantis Story
Continues

[As a child, I dreamed about going into a cave area where the center of the cavern was a lake filled with fish of all types; many other kids were there. This vision took me back to that same place.] I was back in the cave, but I could not find my way. I made the turns I remembered, but I found nothing that reminded me of where I had been or how to find it. I tried to remember something, anything, but nothing that I saw led me back to where I once was.

05/27/94   4:48 a.m.   A Man May Kill His Child as He Prays

I saw this man many years ago, up high in the mountains with his child. He had his hands stretched toward heaven, talking and praying, and in one hand he had a knife with a hooked blade. He talked for a long time, and then he prayed, saying, "I am going to do it." He was trying to persuade himself or trying to prove to the one above that he would do something. This all took place thousands of years ago.

I believe this was Abraham of the Old Testament as he thought he would have to sacrifice his son to Yahweh///.

07/15/94   7:21 a.m.   In the Valley a Great Light

From where I stood I saw a valley with mountains on both sides and thick clouds above it. At its center was a great heavenly light, a brilliant white light with bolts of lightning coming down from the heavens above.

07/16/94   10:50 a.m.   I Start to Remember Where I Saw These Marks ///

I was looking over a case of murder and kidnapping, and the last victim had just left. We knew he was both a victim and in on the crime too. I looked over Dad's clues, remembering something but still not able to put the parts together.

Mama was with me, and I began to see two parts of what happened at this crime scene: I could see what happened before the crime and as it was after it happened—and how Dad found clues. I could hear people talking, the ones who did this crime and the last victim. I heard them talking about killing him, but they changed their minds because he [the victim] was in too deep to tell anyone what had happened. When they brought him into the room, his girlfriend followed. She had been in the car, and if they had known she was there, she would have been killed too. He knew she was there but said nothing. They decided to let him go, and once outside, he got into the light-colored, two-door car that she was driving and lay down on the seat to keep out of sight. The gang members came out, but she had not had time to drive away yet. He was scared, and he told her the truth about everything—his part in it and what really happened.

My father was inside the room where the crime took place and found more clues; Mama and I looked over his shoulder. Mama told me about what Dad did to find clues and what other things he found and how he found them. As we watched Dad, he made three marks on his paper, "///." I said to myself, I know; I now remember where I saw those marks before, and I started to remember everything.

07/17/94   3:54 a.m.   The In-Ardent Word of God///

A voice said these words, and I saw and heard nothing else but this, "The In-Ardent Word of God///."

In the beginning before man and woman, it was all formed, it was made final, and it was made to be forever. It was made from a nothingness, which contained everything within itself that continued and was meant to continue forever. From this, we were all made, but much was made before us, from the same essence as we were, making us offspring of that that came before us in ways we have yet to understand. In the lives of generations before us, and even now, we question where God/// is. The answer: we are more than sufficient to solve all of our problems that really need solving. We have every tool in our spiritual arsenal that can be used in our physical lives. It is not that God/// does not care; it's not that God/// doesn't see the world getting worse by the day. Simply put, we have not developed as we should have, and the world is coming to a crossroads. But we still have time to change things. From the constant cries of our brothers and sisters around the world it may seem like the words from God/// are nonexistent or without caring, but our very essence will never be in danger.

07/19/94   4:50 a.m.   After a Crusade I Was Talking with Some
                           English Gentleman

I was sitting among a group of English gentlemen and ladies after a Crusade, when I was asked about the world's problems. I said, "I know no Scot nor Englishman, no Christian nor Communist, who would not take in and feed a hungry child or person."

The old gent next to me said in my ear, "Do not say anything about Communists," but those words just made me get louder.

I said, "If you speak, speak loud and clear, and if you cannot, then say nothing; but if you say one word, say it loud as if it were your last." A lady, very close by, asked me to sum up everything about her in one word, I did not. They were a little touchy about Communists. I had just gotten back from the Crusades, and my beard was long and I had many needs.

6:11 a.m.   An Assassination

I had just finished my speech standing on a platform before many people, and as I turned around, I saw my lady behind me, looking beautiful and wearing a large white hat. Her lips were as red as the reddest apple. She traveled with me everywhere that I spoke, and as I turned to her, a shot rang out. I just looked at her with my arms open, and I stood there gazing into her eyes. I had just been shot in the back.

6:27 a.m.   Talking May get Me Caught

I was standing, talking with a group of men out in the woods near an open field. It was dusk, nearly dark, and one of the men grabbed me from behind and took me to the ground. He had a cloth over my mouth and he held me there, but I did not fear him because he was a friend. There was complete silence, and I heard out of my own two ears the sound of horses and men on foot coming near. A whisper in my ear said, "Keep quiet, please." I was let go, and I remained silent.

6:57 a.m.   Pray Continuously

I was standing in the dark with three other men, holding staffs in our hands, and I knelt down to pray. As I did, both brothers with me grabbed me by the arms and lifted me up. One of them said, "Come on," and we walked through the door, which opened without our help. Both said to me as we walked, "Pray continuously." We walked through doors that had darkness on both sides.

07/21/94   11:00 p.m.   I Must Raise the Silent Voices of Those Passed On

(a) I was in bed, and as I woke up in this vision, I was told that my duty was to raise the silent voices of all those who had passed on, those whose voices were never allowed to be raised on their own behalf. I saw yellow and black markers, like different types of tombstones, each one with the word "silent///" on it. As I accepted my duty, I found myself lying back in my bed.

The Devil's Workshop and His Helpers

(b) I went to work at a place where there were thousands of reptiles of all kinds—snakes, bugs, dangerous and poisonous, all in different holding cages—and I had to work around them. They were all sizes and colors, sticking their heads out through the wire holding cages. I thought the place used them all for research, but I had not been there very long. I was sitting at my desk when someone walked up and gave me a letter to read. I started to read the letter, but I was called into the office with one other small person for some reason. We sat on the bench, waiting, as the manager came in with another small person who looked exactly like the first one sitting by me. He got up and walked around behind me. I did not move and had no idea what was going on. The one behind me got even closer, and then he put his arm on my shoulder from behind and said something. I did not hear well but did not like it. What he said must have been the wrong thing, because I slammed him to the floor without even getting up. The manager pulled a snake from behind him and threw it on the small person who had walked in with him. These snakes were all different shades of green. As I jumped up off the floor onto the bench to get away from them, the manager began to let out all the reptiles. They were biting the little person all over. Then this all moved to a large arena, where all the deadly reptiles and insects, and some animals, were let loose in one corner of the arena. I was mad at the manager, so I rose up in the air about three feet off the concrete floor that had about twelve inches of water on it and just looked at it all. The creatures moved toward the middle of the arena. I hovered in place and gave an order for all of the reptiles, insects, and animals to move to the other corner and wait. They were slow to react, but they all obeyed except one shark-type looking thing that acted as if it did not hear me. I repeated my command, and he followed all the rest to the other corner. There were men who had been thrown into the arena in another corner. I then moved up in the air about seven feet, and I began to dig a pit in the center of the arena.

I commanded all the reptiles, snakes, fish, and insects to go in the pit. I had the manager and his helper go in the pit too, and I covered it up. As I left the building, I saw the owner of the building come in. He owned the company and the manager worked for him; he knew everything that went on there. I knew him. I had met him before, and I told him that his day would come but it was not that day. He was the one I would have to face someday, but the others I had covered up in the pit, which was brick-lined and the color of brass.

08/06/94   6:08 a.m.   I Am an Apprentice Serving the Master

(a) I was sitting at a table. It was all men, and I had a handkerchief tied around my mouth with a knot in the front. My hair was cut different from the others. I also seemed much smaller than the others at the table. I was sitting to the left of the master and ate. I did not finish what was given to me until all had stopped eating. I got up from the table and cleaned everything that was used to serve the meal. It was all done in silence, as I had been told. There were many others at the table, but the master alone helped me gather everything that was used and had to be cleaned—just he and I.

I Thought I Heard the Voice of God///

(b) At one point, I heard a voice talking low, but in English. I could hardly make it out, but I thought it was the voice of God///, the Creator///, speaking to me. The voice spoke a long time, and no matter where I went I heard it.

This vision tells me to make sure I listen and pay attention to the low voice I hear and know well.

3:55 p.m.   Arctic Ice Will Thaw Soon

I heard a voice say in a low tone, "Arctic ice will thaw soon." I saw nothing and heard nothing else.

08/07/94   7:12 a.m.   Frozen US Gulf Seaport

I was in a gulf seaport looking for something to build with, and a lady named Debra told others and me that we would need to buy a sailboat. The sailboats they were talking about were a little longer in length than I was tall, and they said that I needed it to enter an event of some kind. It seems this is the only way I would be able to get what I needed to build anything was to buy a sailboat I did not want or need.

All this time I was standing on frozen ice; the water has frozen over and it was very thick where I was. I was looking for was materials to build what I wanted.

By 2014, part of the United States gulf coastline will start to show signs of freezing.

9:17 a.m.   Standing beside the One Who Would Judge All Men

I was standing on the shore of a great body of water with the One/// that would judge all men and who would pull out from different sections of the water those men long lost. I was standing in front of a section, and I grabbed a fishing net, dipped it in, and pulled out men. As I pulled them up to the shoreline, they acted as if they did not want to come when first called. He/// said to them, "Get up. You think I did not know you were there?" They did come, muddy all of them, and they were all black men.

Those long lost and seemingly overlooked will be seen and bought into view.

08/23/94   3:17 a.m.   I Saw He Who Held the Dead below Ground

I was lifted up and taken to a place where things caught up with you when you died. I was outside in a large field, and I heard voices calling to me—voices of people wanting what belonged to them, but no one could get it for them, and they had to wait. I walked around that place; it was burial site full of tombstones marking graves and separate burial vaults the size of large rooms in a house for the dead. I understood now what the things were that had not caught up to them yet—they were all the things they had done in life, both good and bad deeds, how they lived and treated others, and even their thoughts. They wanted it to be over and for the scales to be balance or tip in their favor, and they wanted it to happen now. Then I saw the One; he was buried in a burial house but stood as if alive, and I saw him standing in the room, getting dressed as if getting ready for a fight. I saw him eye to eye, and he saw me as he was dressing in an army uniform and equipment, getting ready for battle. I saw him twice, and he was the only one with a body and a soul. I saw him only in the front of the burial house, standing looking in a mirror. The mirror image or reflection of him was what I saw. It ended with me being told and shown everything I had to know about him.

This was a very large burial area, and I saw no people, but I heard those buried there all crying from below the ground. What they wanted was for the things that belonged to them to somehow prove them out. He alone was the cause of this fight that was soon to come.

09/09/94   2:12 a.m.   Some Pages of This Book Are Alive

I wrote many different types pages and assembled them in a book, and some pages were alive physically and inserted into the book in a different section. I had to be very careful with the book, and everything had to be and stay in its proper place.

09/17/94   8:16 a.m.   The Earth Is Burning and One of Its Poles Is Destroyed

I was part of a group that seemed to be all that was left of the earth's inhabitants; everyone else was either dead or gone. We had stayed for the mineral deposits that we could harvest. We all had mental abilities and physical powers far beyond what humans had, and it made it easier to remove the metals from the earth's crust. We removed everything we could for as long as we could stay, working night and day until we had to leave too.

I was sitting at my station, waiting on the others who were digging many miles away, when two of them returned. The earth was burning faster now, but we had one more sign before it came apart. I asked the two who came back what was wrong, they answered, "Nothing." They looked for a tool of some kind. I began to open my mind, and I saw that the tunnel area where they were working had collapsed. I could see the tunnel cave-in would put us three days behind, and I needed to fix this problem myself. I sent small electric charges into solid rock in three places and then a large blast that blew it out nice and neat. Those at the site saw it and went back to work, and those two were sent back to work too.

The time was almost over—the last sign was that everything containing metal was being pulled in one direction. Every metal vehicle was turned over burning, and all were being pulled in the same direction, fast. If you could see it, every metal thing in every city everywhere, was moving in one direction as this earth came to an end.

We, who were there, were made completely different from humans, and we could see and project physical power through our mental processes. We could, at will, do what we wanted, and I was the leader of those still there.

This vision is of a future time when we have learned to move to other worlds, either by our advances or with help from those we always thought existed. We will have a world waiting for us, designed for us.

10/10/94   6:05 a.m.   Three Men Sleep in a Tent While a Boy Sleeps Outside

I saw three men living in a tent out in the woods. They had a boy with them who was treated as if he were an animal, and each one of them would mistreat the boy, making him do all kinds of very bad and dangerous things.

Every night they tied the boy up to a tree as they went to sleep inside the tent, but one night when they tied him up and went to sleep as usual, something happened. Soon they heard a scream from the boy for help, but none of them went to check on him. They heard a terrible noise continue from something that might have been killing the boy, but they never raised their heads or went out to see. The noise from the boy stopped, and they just went back to sleep, but during the night, something came into their tent, it rapped a cord around each of their four fingers without touching the thumb. All three men had their left hands tied with the cord, and when they woke up, all they could see was the cord being pulled through the opening of the tent. That cord was wrapped around each of their four fingers on their left hands, and something was pulling it and them out of the tent.

When justice arrives, it passes over the innocent and takes the guilty, and giving spiritual justice through the left hand.

Book VIII

11/22/94   7:21 a.m.   My Welfare and Adoption

I went to Warrenton and met kids I grew up with when I was only few months to three years old. We had lived at a service station and in a large wooden house off the bypass. My mom and dad used to operate the service station. It was on Routes 29 and 211 west, about a mile before you got into town. We talked about the small bed we used to be put in as kids, about when I started to walk, and about when my parents moved to Gum Springs, Virginia.

There were a lot of small kids my age in our house too, but I found out later that most of us were welfare kids. I remember stumbling into one of the kids before I could walk well, knocking him down. I would find out as I got older that he had a family not far from us up the road. He never forgot me, and now the whole story is open to all that my mother, Margaret Matthews Campbell, adopted me. It was the very best thing that could have happened to me. My friend never forgot that I once hit him with a baby bottle, and I asked him to forgive me for doing that. We remembered all the times we had as kids and even the times when my parents would visit friends and family in Warrenton.

This vision is straight and true. I was born in Warrenton, just outside of town on the bypass for Routes 29 and 211.

11/26/94   6:40 a.m.   Roman Ruler with No Pigmentation of the Skin

I was in a house listening to my mother explain how people cross over from this side to the other side. Right there, in that town, we could see how many had to be taken to the line and made to cross over. At one end of the street was the line, and people waited on the other side for those coming to the line to cross over, but so many did not want to go.

41

This line was only for those who refused to go when their time was up. I saw many Roman Catholic priests in pairs carrying people to the line to cross over. The line was death and payment of sins. There were two or three souls on this side who wanted to stay; one was a man with no skin pigmentation who was dressed like a Roman citizen, and another was a woman with black hair from the same period as the Roman citizen. The Catholic priests wore every color, including gray or silver, and in that town were "angels" [as you call them]—"watchers" who saw everything before and after.

01/19/95   2:00 a.m.   Election Problems for Democrats and Republicans

I like looking at Democrats and Republicans fight in the elections, except this one was different. Everyone was looking in trash cans and other places for certain kinds or pieces of paper. I just stood and watched as both sides looked through everything over and over again. I walked over, looking down into a place with steps going down, and on the concrete floor was a piece of paper. But a man stood near, so I could not get it, and I just went on. They were looking through all the papers and through everything that had anything to do with what they were looking for.

This vision is about the hanging chads in the 2000 election—punch card problem.

01/30/95   11:47 a.m.   Grandfather's Place, Whatever I Thought Was Already Done

We were driving on a dirt road coming out of Grandfather's place in my green Cadillac when I almost ran into what I call a demon. It was animallike with incredible size and was ugly. Then I saw another one that was digging up the whole road, and it really scared me bad. I turned around as fast as I could and drove off the road into a creek where we got out and ran, thinking it was over, but this was only part one.

Next, I was with a vampire-like being, and it was getting everything around me as I ran, trying to find a place to hide from it. I was in great fear and had no idea of what to do to get away. I called the Creator's/// name, but I kept running, and everywhere I ran, it was there already, and whatever I thought I wanted to do, it did it already for me. I finally got away I thought, but I did not know how. It was changing everyone and everything, and I saw it all. It grabbed me and took me up flying, showing me people. They were all white and inside glass containers as if they were frozen in time. I saw women and children, in all kinds of positions, in alcohol being preserved, and I saw human bodies and what they had done to themselves—all looked as if they were caught in time and preserved that way. I saw so many pictures, horrible pictures of people in glass containers filled with a watery-looking substance that I thought was alcohol, which would preserve them forever. Then I sat down by men with bolts of cloth, and I was told I could order clothes from them. I picked up one bolt of cloth but put it back down. One man or king had a suit like it. This area was like where they had sheiks. We continued to look at the people in the glass containers.

This vision concerns me deeply. It tells of a people caught in their ways who are unwilling to change. In our present time, it could be said that many people around the world fall into this category. The demon digging up the road is the infrastructure of a way of life being taken away because we are unwilling to change, and nothing can be done about it because of this present direction, and it is only the start. The white people in jars, as if preserved, are hardened in their ideology so much that no other can exist with them in their present state.

The vampire-like being is actually the blood passed down through the ages to this day; it is also the one I call OneOther that's within me, helping me forewarn people before it is too late, that change can still take place. The belief and faith in things that can be seen, the power of physical things, help make strategic rule of others possible. And yet, it will come to pass when these things—this way of accomplishing the ability to rule—will pass away. OneOther is not my personal darker side but the very knowledge of the ages, which will teach and change me. I, like others, sometimes fear change, but not this time.

02/28/95   4:18 a.m.   OneOther Was Told to Protect That One and Moses

A man who I did not know or see very well, talked to OneOther outside a restaurant saying, "Take care of that one and Moses,"—that one being me. We were playing football in the street in front of the restaurant on Queen and Fayette Streets when the ball got close to the building, and that's when I saw the man talking with OneOther. He said, "In any case, take care of that one and Moses, and that's an order."

This vision is straightforward. It seems to be telling me that as Moses had to face heavy odds, so must I, and going before both of us is the power that will make it possible—guiding us and making the way.

03/03/95   4:57 a.m.   Cain, Abel, and the Woman in the Bible

I was in a living area with my girlfriend when we decided to leave, and on the way out, we met Cain. He smiled at her, and she smiled back at him. I got the idea that these two knew each other. She treated him like she treated me, and I knew that as soon as I left, they would be together. I started to think about that, and I could not let it go. I was very mad. I was not supposed to drink alcohol or eat too much, but I just could not stand what was going on between them behind my back. The only thing I could think to do was to buy some beer and food to drown my pain. I could still see him smiling and looking at her.

03/05/95   6:38 a.m.   A Black Football Player and Golfer

I was walking around the picnic area, looking at all the people having fun. I was headed toward a softball field about a hundred yards away when I saw a young black man pick up a football and throw a tight spiral a hundred yards to a guy on the softball field. I have never seen anybody throw a tight spiral that far before. I was telling a couple of guys about the guy throwing the football, when a golf ball being hit by another black guy almost hit me. I saw a white guy hitting some a long way, but this black guy was hitting them so far that he almost hit me.

I see these two athletes as Tiger Woods and Michael Vick.

05/02/95   6:37 a.m.   The Carpenter Jesus Helps Me

My daughter and I were driving around when we decided to stop and walk a little ways. We joined other people walking into a building to see a program. When it was over, we walked out and started to the car, but we certainly had not realized we were so far from our vehicle. We walked down a back street and across a large open field in the dark. As we walked, two guys came up facing us, and as we walked past them, one of them stopped and turned around; that's when I told Tosya to run. I told her to run and keep on running until she reached the car, and she started to run faster than I had ever seen her run before. I was quite a ways behind her and much slower, but we did get a head start on the guys behind us. I saw where I thought the car was, and I was halfway there. I seemed to get slower and slower until I stopped, and I began to pray right there. I prayed that God/// would help me make sure Tosya was safe, and that I could get there too. I began to run again, very slowly. I reached the last street, and up in front of me was a steep hill. I could see Tosya at the car, but she had no keys to get in. She came back to the top of the hill. I could see her up there, and I also saw a police car, so I knew she was safe. But I still had this hill to climb. I got halfway up the hill but could not go further, so I got down and went around to the other side where it looked like I could climb the hill. Tosya did not have to climb the hill the way I did—she made it a different way. When I went to the other side, I saw some steps off in the distance; each step was high, but I could climb them. As I got closer, I saw some other stairs near me. They did not have as many steps as those in the distance did, but they were still very high, and as I started to climb them, it became more difficult to get up each step. I had to climb them like babies climb steps, but I made it close to the top. Right at the top, as I was about to put my leg over, I saw parts of a wooden roof in my way. That was when I saw the carpenter, and he saw me; he came over, reached down by me, and simply removed the wood parts. He did not physically help me, but he removed those things that were in my way. I finally made it, and Tosya had made it her way, and we both got to the top of the hill.

05/07/95   10:12 a.m.   Denzel Washington

(a) We were told that actor Denzel Washington was supposed to get an award, a Emmy or an Oscar, but it was too early yet.

(b) I saw a group of people arguing about the Emmy or Oscar award someone was supposed to win, and one in the group said, "the horses or dead," and they continued to go back and forth on this.

The discussion in part "a" concerns an award he should have gotten for his pictures, which were in the races with others at earlier times. It was a better picture, but it was not for him then. They just did not want to give it to him then, as was heard, "too early, let's see what else he will do." Then it got a little late, and they realized they should have already given it to him, and they had to find something to give it to him for quickly, so they picked a movie.

05/29/95   3:56 a.m.   I Tried to Get an Upper Hand on Foretelling the Future

I was trying to get to a position of being able to foretell the future. Every step I made, it stayed one step in front of me.

This vision talks about the early '90s, but in the nineteenth year I will get in front of them. The time will be about 2012.

7:52 a.m.   Marks and Symbols All Colors

We were living on North West Street. Mama had just finished washing clothes for the family, and they were piled on a chair in the bedroom. I was just getting out of bed when I noticed that my arms and the backs of my hands were full of marks, slashes, and symbols of all kinds and colors. I called Mama to come and look, to help me understand what these different designs were all about, and she looked but continued with her work. The colors were yellow, red, brown, and green, and both arms and hands were full of them. The colors also went from what I considered to be problem colors to good colors, as if they were an aide of some kind. While all this was going on, I had messed up all the clothes that were on the chair and lost my bathrobe. This all really bothered me when I first saw it.

Right and Left Forearm, Backside

I am not really sure when the marks and symbols started on my hands, arms, face, chest, and maybe other places. My family use to joke about them on my face. The set of hands above are the original markings seen at 7:52 a.m. on May 29, 1995, but these were not the first. I also selected a few photos for the book.

06/11/95   9:20 a.m.   New Military Gas Mask

I was in the army, and I had just arrived on base when I heard a loud alarm. I followed others as they ran to a nearby medical center. Each one drew out a gas mask/suit combination, a new style with other equipment worn around the waist. It was very lightweight but worked well. This combination of equipment and protection, protecting the eyes, nose, mouth, and ears, also came with a communication pack. The complete suits were all regular military issue for our troops as part of their equipment inventory.

Book IX

06/12/95   8:15 a.m.   I Can Do It but Only the Father's/// Way

I was in high school, outside playing, when a schoolmate came up and started to bother me. This boy, Hugh, and another person always bothered me for some reason—day in and day out until I got tired of it and told him exactly what I would do to him. But that did not stop him, and he just continued. It was too much, so I went up the concrete stairs and got up on top of the handrail and stepped off. I was going to jump right on his head, but as I did, I was held in the air above him. I was tired of it; I wanted to go down on him so bad, but I was stopped in midair above him. I cried a lot as I was tired of all this and the treatment I was getting from them, but the Father/// said, "No, you cannot do that even if they hurt you."

06/22/95   2:52 a.m.   The Baby's Touch Causes Me to Vibrate
                            and I See Numbers and Symbols

I was standing inside the house thinking that someone was mad at me, because all of them were looking at me so hard. Maybe it was about the rooster that attacked me. I had to stop the rooster from hurting anyone else, so I grabbed it and shook it until it stopped moving, but I did not think the people there liked what I did at all. They continued to watch me as if I might try to leave. Someone got a black lady from some place, and as she approached I began to hear voodoo drums. This lady was carrying a baby, and they both looked at me as if something was wrong with what I did. She started chanting, looking straight at me very hard. As she walked closer with the baby, she continued the chant, and I started to feel vibrations all over. The vibrations were getting louder and stronger inside me until it almost hurt. She brought the baby to the door where I was standing, never taking her eyes off me, and I wondered what she was

48

trying to do to me. She let the baby touch the floor where I stood, and I started to see numbers, objects, and all kinds of things I had never seen before, and then I woke up.

09/29/95   6:00 a.m.   Ocean City, Maryland, the Water Pulls Away from the Shore

I went to Ocean City, Maryland, and I saw many large dead fish of all kinds floating by. I wanted to go closer and drag one out of the water to get a better look at what happened to it. Then I was standing up on a hill looking at a white young man down below coming out of the water. He walked along the shore, and everything looked normal to me. Later, walking around, I went to the shoreline again, but I saw no water at all. I saw a lot of very deep holes and ruts in the sandy bottom that extended out into the deep empty ocean. I packed up and went home. I told my friends about a place I would like to go fishing, but not Ocean City, Maryland.

11/04/95   8:02 a.m.   A Young Man and an Old Man—Both Dreamers

I went to a convention in a town with many religious people. While walking around talking, I met with the people and pastors from different organizations who had come here on buses from other towns. I was talking with one preacher when he seemed to get angry, and he said to me, "That's what's wrong with some people: you dream too much, you fail to see the realities of life and what is happening in this one." That really hurt me, but I just went on talking to other people that were there. And yes, I was a dreamer.

A year went by, and I returned to the convention. As usual, many people had come back, and an old familiar thing happened again. I heard a young man talking to some ladies, and I heard the way he told them about his faith and what he believed, and it reminded me of myself. Then, across the plaza walked that same preacher going toward the ladies that were just listening to the young man. He said, "That young man is a dreamer, ladies—nothing but a dreamer." He then walked toward me, extending his hand to me. He started to talk about the young man being a dreamer; he had forgotten that just the year before he had branded me a dreamer too.

11/19/95   1:25 a.m.   I Seem to Be Attracting Metal to Me like a Magnet

I was in the living room of my house with a metal flat rod and two shorter pieces, and just by mistake, I found out that the rod was attracting metal objects because I was holding it. It had become a magnet, attracting the two smaller rods yet keeping them at a certain distance, as if creating a magnetic field with me as the source. As I moved the larger rod in a circle, the smaller rods moved away from the larger rod, but moved counterclockwise and at a much faster speed, making their own circle, within the larger circle around me. The smaller rods made a circle within the larger circle, and I felt the vibration from it all. I held the rod by its end, and the smaller rods moved out six feet from the center and moved all around the room. It was getting so fast that I just stopped.

Metal Attracting Device Above

12/24/95   5:42 a.m.   I Am in Spirit Form Talking to a Woman Who Is Crossing Over

I was walking alone, but my steps seemed so slow. It came to me to get off the ground, and I did, but not by myself; I was being led. I saw a dark marble wall, and I decided to go through it. So I cleared everything from my mind and went through. On the other side of the wall I was shown a gold truck. I was also shown the complete outside of a gold-colored house that looked like someone's vacation place. An older white lady stood in one of the doorways. All of a sudden, I was inside, where two men lived in one of two cottages on the property. One of the men I knew. I was in spirit form, and my whole body went up and down the body of the man I knew as if looking at his complete being. I was shown the room and everything around the men for some reason. The men went outside and stood by the gold truck; the name on the side of the truck was Western Electric.

When I followed the men outside, I had a little trouble getting through the glass door. I just could not get through it. I saw them talking, but I could not hear them. Then the door opened, and an older white lady came in. I was standing right in front of her, and she did not see me. I blew a slow breath on her face, and she stopped. She walked on and then stopped again, and she turned and looked at me. She asked me why she was able to see a spirit from the other side. I held her hand and started to talk to her. I told her not to worry. Then the door in front of her house opened, and I knew it was time for me to stop talking. I was going to tell her that in five years many people would see and proclaim their experiences just as she had.

6:52 a.m.   The Same Women in Her Early Years before Her Death

[Here I went through the earlier vision from 5:42 a.m. again, except she was younger.] I was at her house again, and she was younger. I saw her dressed in yellow and gold, and she was very pretty. She looked at me, acting as if she knew me. I asked her if she wanted the portable water fountain I was supposed to bring to her house. It seemed I just showed up, and she smiled and asked how I knew that she needed one. I picked up the fountain, and I knew all that would happen next, just inside her door. The president of a credit union, whom I know, stopped me in the doorway; he wanted some of the water out of the fountain, and I really did not want to give him any of her water, but he had a cup. I stood there while he got some, and she stood there too, looking at all this.

12/27/95   9:21 a.m.   A Mountain Carved-out with Names of Countries on All Its Sides

I was lifted, taken up, and flown to see a gigantic mountain hewed out of molten rock. It was dug out inside, from the center down, and it opened up in a circular pattern like an open cavern with a flat top surface. Its interior shape was fashioned to hold the names of countries of the world on its sidewalls. I was taken in a circle around all this, and I was shown the faces of all the countries on the inside walls. It was enormous.

Next I was in a training barracks in a foreign country, and I decided to go out and run. As I ran for a while, I noticed a man close behind me, so close that he stepped on my heel. He did it twice, so I stopped and tried to talk to him, but he did not speak English. I guessed we were in Germany as he was speaking German. After trying to talk to him for a while, he started to speak English. He said, "See I can speak English," and we started to run again. My dogs, which I brought everywhere with me, were out in front of us as we ran, but after a while I got behind and even had to stop. When I got to the doorway that came out on the mountain, my dogs were waiting for me, and the other runner was at the base or floor of the mountain running around the enormous inner circle. I needed to catch up, so I began to fly up half the interior height of the mountain inside, watching him, but I just got higher instead of going down. I started saying, "Take me down," but I only got higher until the face of the United States on the mountain wall was directly in front of me. As I looked at it, it started to rise up, leaving the level of the other countries, and still rising until it reached the very top.

02/09/96   5:37 a.m.   A Native American Friend Talks to Me
Then the Voice of God/// Speaks

A lady had come to us, talking about a woman I was looking for. She said the woman went down into a deep shaft and did not come out. When we got there, we looked in, but you could only see darkness inside as it angled down. I took a long rope and let it down into the darkness, trying to feel when it hit the bottom. It was like fishing: moving the rope a little one way and then the other to see if something pulled against it. At first, there was no sign at all of anything down there, and then something grabbed the rope, and we began to pull on it. After a long while, I saw a lady's face, but she was scared and let the rope go. I began to talk to this lady, and I let the rope go down inside again to where she was. I told her to grab it, and we pulled her out this time, as well as another lady and the woman I was looking for in the first place.

Then I went to see a Native American friend of mine who had been a chief in his tribe for many years. I did not talk much around him; mostly I just listened to what he had to say. He spoke in his Native American language. I did not understand, but he talked a long time, and I knew what he was saying was for me only. I wanted to understand what he was saying.

Then from the heavens above came the voice of God///, directly above his head. The Father/// said, "Go forth with Me/// as your inspiration and source; build from Me/// your foundation; look back only to Me///; see in front of you, your path, it leads to Me///." Then the Father/// told me about the things that I was taught and had practiced for so long and said that I was to hold on only to Him///.

After that, the Indian chief got down off the porch where he was sitting, passed me, and mounted his horse, riding for a certain length of time. Then he turned and came back to where I was, got off the horse, and went back up on the porch and sat down. He began to talk again for a short while; then he was silent. I knew the distance he rode was a length of time I would have to walk the earth doing what work the Father/// had for me—and walking with power and authority for that length of time. The length was a 360-degree circle, and what I could not understand as the chief talked would be an understanding within me put there by the Father///; I would know and understand at all times my length and authority.

03/26/96   6:02 a.m.   I Have a Set of Keys from All Time Periods

I have a set of keys from every Edmond Campbell (the history of the bloodline) throughout history, keys from every time period, and the knowledge of those keys. Sometimes in our history, knowledge was not shared as it was meant to have been, so I would reclaim the key and give it to someone who would give the knowledge freely to all people.

This vision references the history accumulated in the history of this person's bloodline and spiritual history given by grace from the Father/// to share with all.

03/29/96   5:01 a.m.   Tom Jones—Thank You, Jesus///, for a Rusty Old Voice

I woke up listing to a song being sung called "Thank You, Jesus, for a Rusty Old Voice"; the voice singing it was Tom Jones, the European singing star I have heard and enjoyed many times.

05/27/96   7:23 a.m.   A Genetic Rift in Our Human Structure

I was told simply this: that there was a genetic rift in our human structure, and it was told to me in a way I would not ever forget it.

06/04/96   3:47 a.m.   I Feel Vibrations—Taken Up, I Begin to
    See Alphabets, Numbers, Faces

I was at work, talking to a coworker about certain little things—habits that could help her, like making notes to herself and writing things down in a daily journal. I told her that I did the same thing every day, and I would be lost without it. She left the copy room. Then for some reason I began to feel uneasy, and I wanted to leave too, but as I approached the door, I began to get slower until I could hardly move. The door handle was within six inches of my hand, but I could not grasp it. Then I felt it, vibrations all over my body, and I was being taken up off the floor into a lying position. I was taken through the door without it being opened, and I started to relax, slowing my breathing, and letting it happen. Then everything went dark, and images started to flash before my eyes—images of things, alphabets, numbers, and faces of people. It all lasted a long time.

The vibrations I feel are like a very low electrical charge that acts on every part of my body at once. It seems the vibrations change or act on the physical body, making it pliable in some manner and putting me in a state of mind or of awareness where things can happen—like the ability to accept knowledge at a faster rate and retrieve it when the time is right or when I am able to properly understand it.

07/05/96   1:27 a.m.   Three Books Lay on My Path, One Opened

Walking along a path, I saw a large open field to my left. I then saw three books lying on the ground, and the smallest one was opened. I passed them by, because I thought they were religious books from some company or a training course of some kind. I passed them and something began to happen; a stream of light hit my left ear very fast, and a high-pitched hum started and lasted for a long time. I could not get it to stop. When I got home, I went straight to bed, and as I dosed off to sleep, I began to see faint things passing before my eyes. I could not tell what they were, but after a while, I could see that a lot of them looked like Greek building structures with close columns all in a row. While lying there, I could feel my wife's hand under me; I was hoping she would not cause me to wake up. She did not, and I continued to see those structures.

The three books on my path are the same as the three envelopes (see March 28, 1986), and the open book is this book reduced from 475 visions to 260. The open field tells me what the books really consist of and to my left tells me who is giving them to me. The high-pitched hum is the actual information being downloaded to me.

07/07/96   12:35 p.m.   My Father Asked Me "Which One Was Made"

I spoke to my father, and he asked me this question: "Which one was made?" I did not understand clearly what he was asking me—it did not make sense to me. The question I thought was, "When was man made?" I said, "Last," but he was asking a specific question about man.

07/11/96   6:12 a.m.   A Young Lady Dressed in a Santa Suit Has Car Trouble

[I saw this as it happened in the life of this young woman on her way home in 1994 during Christmas.] The woman had car trouble and stopped at a service station for help. She found the attendant, but there was a little communication problem. She was wearing a complete Santa's suit and had to take off the mask to talk to him. He was surprised to see a woman wearing the suit, but he repaired the car, and it was over and she was on her way home.

The next year, the same women had car trouble in the same place and went to the same service station for help. It was during the Christmas holidays again, and she played Santa again, but this time the problem was a bit more serious. She had a harder time convincing the attendant to help her this time, but his last words were to her "I will help you," just as he had said before.

I was telling this story to a group of people, most of who were the same people I told it to last year. When it got to what the problem was with the car and how it turned out, I said, "No, stick around, and you will find out—you will just have to wait until next year."

However, I will tell you now. From year to year we continue to do the same thing, and we end up in exactly the same place; for some reason we do not seem to want to change our circumstances.

07/23/96   5:57 a.m.   The Spirit of a Man and Women and Two Hundred White Horses

I was running, trying to get away or hide from those behind me. I ran into a man who looked like a spirit, and he said, "When I died, twenty white horses came to get me." I left him quickly and ran into a church, and its entrance was below ground in the basement. I hollered at the entrance door. The glass was broken, and no one was there, but a woman who looked like a spirit said, "It's closed," and then she said, "Two hundred white horses came to get me when I died." I left her in a hurry too.

08/17/96   4:52 a.m.   At the Metropolitan Museum of Art and I Cannot Pass through Its Walls

I was walking along and decided to take a dirt road that led out of town. As I walked down the road, two young men were walking behind me. One of them called me a name not my own, and I was not supposed to hear, so I just walked faster to get ahead of them. My speed became much faster. They were on the other side of the road, and I continued to get faster in my steps until I felt like lifting off. I became airborne. It was night, and the first thing I saw was the ocean and clamshells, and I knew I was not alone; I was being carried.

I started to see a very large city, I think was New York, and then I saw the ocean again. We continued to travel so fast. As I looked back, I think I saw New England. All the way as we flew, nothing was said at all between us. For a short distance, it was as if we traveled through a mix of air and clouds turning in weird directions, and when it cleared, I saw another large city again. We now traveled from the ocean into the city, and from the style of all the buildings, I thought it was England.

I saw that the one carrying me was female, and she took me to a museum for some reason. When we first got there, we just looked at the front of it for a while. The front was made partly of glass, with walls that were covered with very old cloth; the designs on them were made in the form of an Egyptian tablet from more than three thousand years ago. It reminded me of a Greek design. We went in as usual, by passing through the wall or whatever it was, but we just bounced back—we couldn't get through. We could not get through this quilted wall made of concrete. It had never happened to me before. Concrete was no problem to go through. The design on the wall was the problem. That's when I asked if this was the Metropolitan Museum of Art, because the structure looked Greek to me. Not getting through any type of structure had not happened since the '80s, and an old-fashioned screen door caused that. This wall structure stood for something or guarded against something.

The museum in this vision is in England, but it is the equal of the Metropolitan Museum of Art. I cannot pass through it because I think something is wrong inside it.

09/29/96   4:18 a.m.   Two Young Girls Are Very Old in Spirit

We were in the dorm room at college, and the men and women lived and dressed in the same room but had separate showers. I walked into the room and headed to my bunk when I noticed two women getting dressed. I noticed, but I did not even look in their direction. As I approached my bed, I noticed someone was hiding under the spread that draped over the side of the bed. I touched the head of the person, a little person, and two girls got out from under the spread and stood up. One said, "How did you know it was us?" I smiled as we talked. The room started to fill with people, and she asked me if there was anything that I needed, or anything I wanted her to take back to the Father///. I knew these two little girls, one seven and the other three. Both were from the Father/// and had made the visit at His/// request. I said, "Everything is fine, but keep it coming." She said, "You want me to say it loud?" And I said, "I know it doesn't have to be loud, but yes, say it a little loud." The three-year-old stood there, looking up at me, eyes gleaming, never leaving the older one's side. I felt an emotion that overwhelmed me. So I knelt down and hugged them both as if I had known them for thousand years, and I had. She laughed and kept her beautiful smile. She had just come to visit in person—just two young ladies, but so very old in spirit.

10/3/96   7:54 a.m.   A Lawyer for the Judge Advocate
                          General's Corps

I was a lawyer in the army's Judge Advocate General's Corps, and because of the war, I had a job to do. It all started during a war when young men and women fought from behind bushes and trees in large forest area for a long time. Young people fought this war, ages from sixteen to thirty-five years old, and many of them were still dying even to this day because of it.

All I could remember was when you were a sniper you shot at the smallest glimmer of sunlight cast by any object, usually it was a rifle turning its sights on you are or your comrade, and you had only a second to turn, point, and shoot. That's what I did, that was my job for a long time, until one day I saw a shadow that was too close, and I knew I was not fast enough this time. I do not remember anything else.

As a lawyer, I heard some soldiers had been jailed for not fighting, for giving up. But it was more than that—something happened out there that made both sides give up. When the officers in charge got to the front lines, soldiers on both sides were sitting together, guns thrown down away from them. They had just decided to stop the fighting and killing of each other.

I was in a spirit form as I looked down from above it all, and I saw in the hearts of those sent to fight that they were raised to love life, all life, anyone's life, and not to take life. They were being forced to fight against their beliefs and the Creator's/// words, "Thou Shall Not Take Life///," not sometimes, not ever. In war, abortions, and prison death sentences—you simply become that which you fear or hate. On Earth, we think of self, but we must move to a higher plane of understanding, of caring, of hope, of knowing, and when we do, we add love and goodness to all of creation. Fear of dying either makes you a murderer or frees you from the bonds of this place of spiritual trials—but not bodily trials. You must rise above this and do only what is told of you. Love the Creator///, love thy mother and father, and love thy neighbor as you love yourself. Take nothing you would not want taken from you, live above the physically expected realities, and prove to the Creator/// who you really are. Do not bother with the other physical beings that walk around in the same actor's scene as you.

I was in my office, and I heard that those who had given up needed legal counsel. My commanding officer thought we would be crazy to take the job, but I was taking the job. I headed to the place where they were being held to give them the best defense I could.

When I got there, I was told that a young soldier was told by his commanding officer to go to the front lines and take the place of soldiers who were killed. He did as he was told, and that's when it all started.

Someone was killed who would not take a life. A young female soldier had waited to be killed, because she was not going to take life; and it all happened after that.

10/05/96 7:16 a.m. Beautiful Day, Silence, No Sounds at All, and Then One Here and One Gone

I was taking in the view, looking at a bright beautiful sunny day. I watched two kids playing together; then one was gone, and the other was still there playing. I saw two young people about twenty years old, a male and female; he pushed the female and then he was gone, and she lay back as if everything was okay. I saw lots of others, two together, and then one there and one gone. Before this started to happen, it was a beautiful day. The wind was blowing and then it stopped. No noises of any kind—just silence—no wind blowing, everything stopped. And then it started: one person here and one person gone. It was happening everywhere.

10/25/96 3:58 a.m. I Am Flying, the One Carrying Me Talks to Me

I was outside, and it was dark as I looked up into the night sky. For some reason I wanted to jump up as if I wanted to fly. I did, and the next thing I knew, I was going up. I felt arms around me, real arms from someone behind me. I continued to go up, looking at the sky, the stars, and the little lights that shot off like fireworks. Then the one carrying me said, "Relax, you are always so tense." This was the first time the one carrying me ever spoke to me, and it was a female voice. She gave me a schedule of things, and said, "We will do this today and Monday." I simply relaxed as she talked, and it was over.

I was lying in bed. I saw a woman at the dresser on her knees going through a drawer; she thought I was asleep. I wiped my eyes to make sure I was not asleep or dreaming. I slowly moved toward her, reaching out to grab her. I got her and was holding her down on the bed, and that's when I saw it was Ann, someone I knew years ago. She started to tell me something about why she was doing that, and I saw she had no clothes on from the waist down. She held one leg high up in the air, exposing everything, and I told her to put her leg down.

After a while I went into the kitchen to find something to eat. I decided to cut up a pineapple but I really wanted something else. Out of the clear blue sky, the guy next door brought me a plate covered with plastic wrap; it had mashed potatoes, gravy, peas, and meatloaf—just what I had wanted.

This seems to be in three parts. The first part I actually made moves with the idea of seeing stars and other objects in the sky; I got an immediate answer. In the bedroom, the young woman had her leg up, and I told her to put it down. Is that really what I would do? In the kitchen, I settled for a cut-up pineapple, but that was not what I really wanted. I must watch out for and be aware of earthly temptations if I want to soar.

7:18 a.m.   I Traveled with a Young Speaker and Teacher

(a) I was only a witness to this; it happened long ago and how it will turn out is still in question. I was with a young speaker, teacher, and leader. He was somewhere in his late twenties to about thirty years of age, and he traveled with many others. They heard and trusted in the words he shared with them. One day as he walked with them, he was captured and held for murder and robbery. The others with him just looked on, except one, who remembered him saying to those who followed and listened to him, "I have a destiny, and all of you who have heard and watched me should know this." He said it repeatedly to those who followed him, "I have a destiny." I looked down on all of this happening so long ago.

(b) I was witness to this also: there was a young woman, known as a woman of the streets, and her father was part of a team that entertained people. His whole family had a history of entertaining people everywhere they went, but this one day she was caught and had no family to run too. She had no way out and it ended with her being stopped by others and accused of wrongdoing.

The above vision is about Jesus and Mary, one of his disciples.

11/1/96   3:45 a.m.   I Hid My Things in Holes on the Sides of
the Mountain

I lived in a cave on a mountain rock face, just under the cliff overhang, and I used the holes in the rock face to store and hide my belongings. I would stand on top of this mountain and along the edge of it, looking at everything around it and thinking about the creatures crawling in the holes where I had my things.

This vision is in the time of Jesus and before.

4:54 a.m.   Talking to a Lady Who Said God/// Had Left Her

I was talking to a lady over the phone, and she told me her heart was broken, and that God/// had left her, and she could feel the difference. I told her, "Don't ever worry about God///, our Creator///, leaving you alone, for there has never been a day when God/// was not with us, watching you and your development and growth. When you feel alone, pray—pray saying a new prayer of your own making, knowing God/// made all things within creation. We talked a long time until she became silent, with my voice fading in and out at times as I continued to talk to her.

11/16/96   6:47 a.m.   Rag Dolls Stuffed with Cut Diamonds

This young woman had a vision about her father asking her what her favorite thing in the world was as a kid, and she said her rag doll. She was at a stage in her life where she needed help, financial help, in the worse way, and I just happened to be there. She jumped me, right on my back with joy, telling me her vision, and then she went to get her rag doll. She had no idea it was stuffed with diamonds from the time she was a kid.

Book X

11/25/96   2:01 a.m.   A Bed with the Head of a Cobra on It

I was standing, looking at pictures in very dim light, and I sensed this was an ancient artifact with an Egyptian background—a bed with a headboard that had a head of a cobra on it. There were pictures on walls of drawings and symbols, and all these things flashed by in only seconds. The room was filled with ancient symbols and charts.

12/03/96   4:47 a.m.   Two Beings, One with the Head of a Light Beacon and one with a Sword

I had a garage in the one hundred block of Harvard Street in Alexandria. One day while I was there, something happened that I couldn't explain, and I can't even now. I had several employees working with me, and as they came in that morning to work, I walked out front to look around. When I looked up toward Cameron Street, I saw two beings at the end of the street, the likes of which I had never seen before. One was sitting in a chair, and one was standing in front of him. The one in the chair had a light beacon on his head, and he looked in one direction only: straight up the street where I was. In front of this being stood the other with a sword in his hands, also looking in one direction: at me. The one sitting with the light beacon on his head was moving it side to side, while the one in front of him stood fixed. Both were looking in my direction. Every day the two were there, at the end of the street.

One day, we got a van in the shop to work on. I was not sure where the van came from, but no one in the shop could work on it. I called in a mechanic with special talents to do the repair, and when he arrived, he went right to work on it. He pulled the van into the bay and worked on it for a long time. Every so often, I would ask him how he was coming along on it, and his answer was, "It is coming." Then all of a sudden he backed part of the van outside, and as I looked at it, it seemed he had separated it into two complete vans. I saw him separate the outer shell from the inner shell and slide it out of the garage. There sat a faded yellow van, and the van pulled from it was different shades of beautiful yellow.

I moved both vans away from the garage and parked the yellow van in back, up on a little hill where I had cars. Then I moved the cars closer to the shop.

I was not sure what was going on, or what was wrong with the van, but I had never seen anything like that before. Those two down the street could have had something to do with all of it—the inner and outer shells.

Let me explain the last part first. Everyone has heard this: the van gives me the answer to the two at the end of the street and what they mean as far as I am concerned. The inner van is pulled out of the shell, which is probably understood by everyone as the two parts of one's self. The two at the end of the street means the two sides of a person, one bringing the light or understanding, and the one with the sword representing power and authority that can be used if needed; the two parts of the same being, acting independently if necessary.

12/13/96   5:45 a.m.   A Buddhist Monk Heals a Man with a Growth on His Back

I was present when a Buddhist monk talked with a man who had a very large growth on his upper back, and I saw the monk talk with the man for a short while and then begin to pray. I then saw the very large growth become a man of wood, and the monk grabbed it and showed the man who had been carrying it for so many years exactly what it was.

12/25/96   7:45 a.m.   Two of Us, He Breaks the Back of the Army and I Will Do My Part

There were two of us playing our parts: he as the fighter, the one that was supposed to break the back of the armies, and I as the one who would not hurt a fly. We both worked together, yet apart, doing whatever needed to be done. This time we were fighting a woman, as she ruled and had those who served her (who were neither man nor demon but in between the two) fighting with her. We fought them; my partner cut one several times, but it would not die. We knew it would take a special weapon to finish that one, and we had them. My partner went off, running behind another one, and I inched closer to the first one. When the time was right, I would do my part.

This vision is similar to the vision dated December 3, 1996; it is the same being as the one in the chair that had a light beacon on its head and the one that had a sword in his hands. The two beings actually represent the two part of one body.

8:45 a.m.   Hands, Praying and Clapping, Pointing the Way

I lifted my head, and I saw a wonderful thing. It was hands in every size, color, and shape, and they were together as if in prayer and then clapping and pointing the way. Just hands only as far as you could see. I did not see anything else but hands—all sizes, colors, and shapes.

01/03/97   8:17 a.m.   My Death and Rebirth

I was in a room on my back, and I was looking up at a jade green ceiling. I had no movement of my body, and I just stared at the ceiling until it seemed to move, or I moved toward it. I seemed to be getting closer and closer until it was about two feet away from my face. I thought about stopping, but I knew I must go all the way. I continued to stare until the ceiling was only inches away from my face, and it seemed that something in the lower part of my head and upper neck area snapped.

It snapped, and I was still on my back looking at the ceiling but in another phase. I began to see light, a small amount, and then it grew. I could see it was coming from a door with a window. Still on my back, I was looking up and back over my head at the door and light as I moved toward it on air. I thought in mind to open the door as I got near it, but it did not open. And then it came to me: try to move, and I did very slowly. I turned the doorknob and opened the door, still on my back as I went outside.

Then I found myself in or on a baby carriage with a baby, and the baby made some kind of remark about me. I said, "What did you say?" and the baby said something else.

I see and feel myself pass from one life into another, and the baby is my next body but the baby is in charge. I am OneOther, and the baby could very well be Edmond, just the two of us now.

11:56 a.m.   He/// Who Sees All Gives Me an Ability to See

He/// who sees all, blew into the eyes of a young boy and deferred judgment until the end.

I have been given the privilege and ability to witness and speak within the authority given me by my Father/// concerning the world and where it stands at this time. It is with the understanding that some mistakes will be made, but I know that everyone who has ever been on earth has to account for their space and time.

01/22/97   4:41 a.m.   A Baby in Spirit Form Grabs Me and Holds On

I got into the elevator at work, and something grabbed me from behind. It was a child, a baby, a spirit presence in the form of a child. It held on to me, and as the elevator went up, I talked to it and held its little hand, asking how it felt. We continued to talk, and I noticed the elevator had cobwebs in one corner of it. We just continued to talk.

02/07/97   4:24 a.m.   Two Asian Armies Facing Each Other

I was in an Asian country, in the body of an Asian army soldier, facing men of another Asian army at their border. I tried to talk, but the soldiers facing us started to extend some type of mechanical device onto our side. I was alone. I knew that this device was filled with some type of aerosol spray or gas that was poison. They extended it about a hundred feet, and I tried to disrupt what they were doing. I started to run, but I did not get very far before it caught up to me. It was a yellow mist, and when I smelled it, it was over. It was two Asian armies on their borders.

02/16/97   4:56 a.m.   New Training Method

I was in a room in bed when in walked a young woman named Helen who I went to elementary school with, and she started to dust and straighten up things in the room. I told Helen to come lay down, and after a while, she did, but she soon left. I began to get instructions on how to view the four screens that were at the foot of my bed. The four large screens had smaller screens in each of them, and it was like looking at television in a classroom. I was alone, and at first I watched all four screens at the same time because they seemed to be working as one, with one image. And then a little man appeared on the screen. I was told to pay attention whenever the little man appeared and track him as he went from screen to screen doing his thing. At the same time, other things were happening, on all the screens or sometimes on just one, but they happened independently from the little man.

Before I saw all this, I saw all the screens fill with numbers and alphabets, a million of them going past like a computer. The movie-like image filled all four screens, and then the little man appeared. After it was over, I got up and went outside my room where there was an elevator, and I got on it.

In the elevator was a beautiful young woman who I knew, and she was sitting down on something in the corner. As I walked toward her to talk, I reached for her hand, and she looked at me and said, "You are from the fifth floor, right?" And I said yes. She knew me and about me, and as I kissed her, she said, "We will be in the lobby in a minute." I said to the elevator, "Stop in the middle between floors." The elevator stopped, and she looked at me saying, "How did you do that?" And I said, "I talk to them." She stood up, and her head almost hit the elevator ceiling. She said, "There is a camera in the ceiling above us recording our every move." I said, "Camera, erase your film for the last few minutes." We kissed again, and she said, "I should have stopped by your room." Then the elevator started to fall fast, going floor by floor. She was scared until I said, "It's all right." I told her, "The elevator is simulating a malfunction, a cause for the stopped elevator and erased film, so when they check it will be written up as a malfunction or electrical problem." The elevator slowed and returned to my floor. As I started to get out of the elevator, she said, "You are that preacher," and I would not say anything to that.

When I was watching the screens before, I had on glasses that I removed a couple of times to see what difference it would make, and if it was better with or without them. The glasses gave color to the screens, and without them, it was only black and white. Hillary and Helen, two friends of mind from North West Street, came in one behind the other, and Hillary started to move my pillow around. As I stood there waiting for her to finish and leave, she put my pillow on the floor. I did not like that at all—dust and dirt were getting on it. She finally left, and that's when Helen came over to the bed. It all reminded me of the three women many years ago who taught me how to ride my bicycle with its ten speeds.

02/22/97   6:12 a.m.   Drive Gear Radar Imaging System for Vehicles

I was riding in a very large vehicle, sitting up on top in a compartment separate from the main part of the vehicle that held the load. I was sitting in water up to my waist, with my mind on first getting and then counting silver coins hidden under a clear plastic sheet on the floor where I sat. Every once and a while I wanted to look around and see the countryside that we were traveling through. As we drove along, I could hear the heavy breathing or shortness of breath of our driver over our intercom system; she needed to lose a little weight. After being on top and wet, I went down inside the personnel compartment. This vehicle was the largest of its kind.

Then there were only three of us with this vehicle, our female partner had gone, and I was in the control center compartment where we had a specific place to sit. I looked around, thinking about Vietnam, and I ended up telling them a joke about two men in a truck, high on pot, each thinking the other was driving the vehicle. I asked the person next to me who was driving this truck, because I could see the three of us, and we were not driving. He pointed to the control system and said, "That's driving." It knew where we came from, where we were going, and the construction of the roads, and all of our surroundings were recorded on a hard drive in its system.

02/23/97   4:15 a.m.   Black Guy Playing Golf in His Hotel Room

I was in a bedroom where I was making up the bed. One end of the bed was made the old-fashioned way with old used things and 90 percent of the bed was made my way. I lay down for a while, then I got up and remade the bed. Two guys started to hit golf balls, and I backed away and just watched. Golf balls were on the floor everywhere, and they were hitting them up on the bed; they acted as if the bed was the green, and getting it up on the bed was a winner. I saw this black guy playing, and to me, he tried to cheat, and the other guy let him get away with it I think. Then I saw him kick his ball because this was a bad place for him; the bedroom floor was the fairway, and the bed was the green.

A pro golfer and his caddy playing golf in his hotel suite.

5:15 a.m.   All My Visions Were on Display

I was in a very large building with tall ceilings where I saw all my visions on display along with the starship Enterprise. The Enterprise was first, and then all the other visions, large and small, were hanging from the ceiling of this very large building. I just stood there looking up at them, and the Enterprise was so large.

02/24/97   4:15 a.m.   My Boys—Three, Five, and Seven Years Old

My family and I were out in a grassy marsh area for some reason. I had three kids with my wife, and the boys were three, five, and seven years old. I called out in a hurry, because my smallest son was caught under a glass container made with two inner rings. My son was inside it. I was afraid a snake had bitten my son. I saw one snake lying in about four to six inches of water not far from the container. For some reason I did not rush to take him out and away from the other snake that was inside the container with him. I saw what looked like a rattlesnake in one section of the container, and my baby was in the other. I was trying to figure a way to separate them before I removed the container. The boy looked okay, and he cried, wanting to get out. Finally, I was able to run off the large snake lying in the water near the glass container. I decided to lift the glass container up where my son was, but first I tried to make my son and the snake relax. As I lifted up the container and grabbed my boy, the snake moved away. I put my son down, and he started to play right away, but I did not want him to go very far from us again.

I told the five-year-old to go get him, and the five-year-old tried to catch him, but I had to help trap him. That boy was fast. As I picked him up, I saw a wound on his arm. As I looked closer, I saw it was a snakebite. He seemed fine and had no reaction to the bite at all, but we headed to the hospital anyway.

11:39 a.m.   Flying Over the Rocky Mountains Alone

I was flying over the Rocky Mountains on my own; I was going very fast and was very high up when I started to lose altitude and come down. I was still going very fast, but I did not have control. I started to pray that I would not crash into the mountain, because I did not think I could survive that. As I got closer to the mountain I was going fast. I cleared it and started to see the ocean, but I continued to have no control over my speed.

The whole area looked wet and rainy, like Washington state with the trees and the cool damp conditions. I felt as if I was going to hit the water, and I was still going too fast and could not get control at all.

Then it changed. I was still going fast but against traffic on a four-lane highway. I was still trying all types of positions to slow down and get some control. I finally slowed a little, but it was still too fast. I was trying to get my speed down to the speed of the trucks on the road. Just then Tosya called me, and I woke up.

03/25/97   6:40 a.m.   Jesus/// Answers Questions

I was looking at men questioning Jesus/// about something as He/// stood beside a wall where many others were. Along this wall men stood at floor level, on top of the wall, and at every point from bottom to top. This was just a wall standing alone—it did not support anything at all; maybe it once did, but it was only a wall, with nothing else around it or above it. As they questioned Jesus///, He/// told them something and started a count-off by saying "one." The next man said "two" and so on until every man on the wall was accounted for including himself. I do not know what questions were posed to Jesus///, but they all were included in the final count.

03/28/97   3:37 a.m.   I Went Below to His Place of the Dead

I was at home and a friend of mine had just died, and it seemed that people were leaving fast—dying, going before their times for some reason; it was as if someone gave them approval to die. There were so many, and I knew some of them, and some of them were close to me. Then I went below to this place of the dead. I lay there and the ones in this place started toward me as I arrived. I knew they would know the difference when they touched me, because I was warm, not cold. I had been sent to see what was going on in this place of the dead.

Two came to me: one of them was warm and the other cold. The warm one was in charge and wanted me to get to work; he did not know me. I started to work, and they had no trouble from me. In one area I saw a woman I knew. She had needles sticking in her back, which was a reminder to her of her past life. I wanted to see how people were being treated in this place—it was the reason I was sent.

After a while, the place started to have more and more people in it. They had all rushed their deaths for some reason. That's when I saw a little boy, and he had not made the change. I said, "What are you doing here?" He said, "I am with my grandfather." The grandfather was supposed to come, but not the little boy. Then I was called—a woman had come down and was standing in the doorway, calling me by my name. I answered, "Yes," and she said, "They want you back upstairs now." (See also August 23, 1994.)

04/08/97 4:02 a.m. Arabs and Jewish People Want Me to Help but Will Not Help Each Other

I was walking to a meeting when I saw a man I knew coming out of a house. He was mad, very mad, and he looked at me and told me not to go that way. He looked as if he wanted to hurt me very bad. I passed him on the way to a meeting with some Arab and Jewish people. OneOther was with me as usual. When I reached the meeting place and entered, I found out right away that they wanted to help me but did not want to help each other—and yes, they all acted like the first man. I continued to talk as I had for some time, telling them about the first man and what I knew about him.

I went back that way and I saw and met some young men who threatened my life. As we talked, I felt the same rage and hate in those three that I did at the meeting. During the meeting, I continued to think about the first man I met and the first house I saw on the way there. As I talked it seems to do no good, they wanted to help but would end up killing the helper. It was as if they cried for help, but at the same time they were saying, "Stay away. Please help us, but if you do, we will kill you."

04/21/97 11:55 p.m. Hotel—Spirits in My Room as I Lay in Bed

I was in a hotel room, in bed, but very scared, because I was asleep when I felt something moving the covers and feeling me. I started to pray fast and hard. I finally got the light on, but I was still scared as I noticed two very large footprints on the floor, large and deep, as if whatever was there weighed a lot. I could actually see the carpet being crushed down as it walked. Then, to my rescue came some men talking to me as I lay in bed, talking and walking the room over, trying to find or see something. They asked me to tell them where it was, and then they figured out it was right at my bed, lying beside it. They asked me to talk to it as they tried to measure its size.

I began to talk to it, and as I did I started to see different figures in an old-style chair near the wall. The first figure I could only make out as a cloud or mist. The second was a young white girl about fourteen or fifteen years old. She looked straight ahead, as if looking at something, and then she turned her head to talk to me. She said something I could not hear, so I asked her to say it again. She did and this time I faintly heard her, but the others in the room heard nothing and saw nothing. I called to her again, and this time I heard the last words she said: "my mother some flowers." The first part I still did not understand. This all happened on one side of my bed, and then it started up on the other side but stopped.

After a while, the men left and two young boys came in, who looked to be six and eight years old. I asked them if they were going to stay, and the older boy said, "Yes." All this time I was still in bed, looking at all this. One part of the room was a set of universal weights, and the smallest boy had one of the weights, which he dropped on top of one of the large footprints. For a while, the large footprints were gone, but they came back, I noticed them by my bed, and the boys were running around the room, often passing them without noticing them or stepping on them. The boys pulled out their bed right by the footprints and I saw it move back and forth, and I was still a little scared.

05/01/97   5:02 a.m.   AT&T and Bell Atlantic Have School Programs

I went out to a school to get copies of some materials left there by AT&T for the kids. The telephone company had taken equipment to schools to show kids their programs and to teach them how they worked. They wanted to help these kids and give them firsthand knowledge of their new programs and equipment for the future. The telephone companies, including Bell Atlantic and others, had all done this; the problem was none of them came to our school to give our kids a head start and a better chance in life. I showed my friend the information I got, one page, both sides, and two other pages, both sides—all showing the school faculty how the program worked. I was hurt that they did not include our school, so I was going to contact them as soon as I could to get them to consider our school.

05/24/97   6:32 a.m.   My Mother Comes Down from Above and Tells Me All about My Future

I was at home in bed, but this bedroom was one I did not recognize. I was looking at a new water container that I did not know how to work. It was supposed to give me all the cool water I wanted to drink as long as I needed it, but I might not have set it up right. Mama came into the room from above, from the Father///, as she had many times before when she thought she needed to. I was sitting on the side of the bed, looking at her, and she was dressed so beautifully in white, gray, and black with white under it, and her hair was just flowing in the air.

She began to talk to me, and at the same time she assembled the water container. She told me many things, all having to do with what I thought my future was. She finished the water container, but it sometimes gave out too much water at once, so she made some adjustments to it. Then she introduced me to a man who began to talk to me about faithfulness to one, and all the problems it could bring if you failed. He said he had failed in loving the one he most cherished, and he felt he was being punished, even now in his present state. So now he went wherever he could, warning others. He was warning me of this fate and what could happen if I failed as he did. He looked like a guilty man, as if every minute he was paying a price for his mistakes.

All of this first began as I sat on the side of my bed thinking about how many spirit beings had come to me in the past and touched me or covered me completely. The number is three—three different forms but many, many times.

The Water Container

The top of the water container was turned upside down full of water, but only gave drops down into the lower container where I filled my cup, and it was ice cold all the time.

Mama finished the water container, and the man who had come with her finished talking with me, but he seemed to be suffering so I began to talk to him. I told him that he had been sent to me in his present form to show me and to make me understand the importance of choosing one and keep that one and not committing adultery. I then told him that he was sent just to talk to me and to show me, and that his soul spirit was not there but above in heaven, safe and free. All this was for me, and he was not really suffering at all.

06/01/97   7:12 a.m.   Shoes with Batteries That Keep Our Vital Signs

I was at work, and my shoes needed batteries in them because they sent out continuous information about us at all times throughout the day. It sent out our vital signs and our present location to the office, where continuous records were kept on each of us.

06/16/97   12:21 a.m.   Lifted Up and Taken by an Invisible Spirit Form

I was lying in bed when something sat on the foot of my bed. I got scared and said something, and it got up and went away. I knew right away that I should not have done that, and so I said I was sorry, and after a while it came back and sat down again. This time, the weight on the foot of my bed tilted it in that direction. Then I felt vibrations; I felt myself being taken level on my back and then taken somewhere at a very fast speed. There was a feeling of speed, but in a short time it got faster, and then it was like a three-speed transmission: the speed got even faster until I ended up in a classroom. The classroom was full of students talking about the right thing to do and their beliefs. I could not hear very well. The classroom was dimly lit, and that was not good. I heard very little. We were all seated when I heard someone say that Ray Charles's seat was empty.

07/14/97   5:17 a.m.   A Spiritual Presents Follows Me Everywhere

I was with members of my family, and we had a serious problem: a spirit presence was following us everywhere we went, and it did not seem to make any difference how fast we traveled in our vehicles. At some point, it caught up to us, and we were on the run again, trying to get away. As we drove, we sometimes saw it behind us at different angles. It had been after us for a long time, and it was always there, it never gave up. It bothered me very much; I prayed all the time that it would leave us alone, but it never did. No matter how fast we drove, it got closer. We had gained some distance on it, so we stopped for a short time, but before we could start moving again it caught up to us. My family called me, and as I moved toward them, I went right through it. It lifted me up in the air above everyone, and I started to pray for everyone and everything to be forgiven. Then I heard my daughter call me, and I came back down and it was gone. Everyone wanted to leave there fast.

07/27/97   9:57 a.m.   A Palace Set Down Inside of a Mountain Where Elephants Go

I was with others, flying in a plane over a palace in a country that I did not know. I saw thousands of elephants on the mountains surrounding the palace below. Then something happened, and we were forced down. We were able to land and escape into the top part of the palace, but they got the boy who was with us. We were on the ledge or corner of the building, and I saw something that I did not understand.

Hundreds of elephants were coming down the sides of the mountain all around the palace—all at one time, as if they were going into the palace. The palace sat hundreds of feet down inside the mountain with no visible paths, roads, or other way to get down to where the elephants wanted to go. In front of the palace was a large body of muddy water, and the rest was just a rocky surface. I could see that the gate to enter the palace was opening slowly. The elephants tried to come down the side of the mountain, but they got only a short way down; they could not find places to put their feet. I saw them get down on their knees and just give way and roll down the mountain the rest of the way. Some of them hit the muddy water. They all got up and went in the entrance of the palace. More came down the same way from different heights on the mountain. There were no people around anywhere at all except for us.

The boy was still missing, and the army was looking for all of us. I just lifted off the roof ledge and began to fly up very high, looking completely around the outside of the palace. I saw the boy—I saw him in a window of the palace—and I flew through it to get him. I found the royal family hiding there too.

08/08/97   4:05 a.m.   Taken to a Room Where I Pick Up Nails

(a) I was sitting on the couch with my father as others entered the room. Dad got up and went upstairs, and I continued to lay there. Tosya, my daughter, was very young, maybe three or four years old, and decided to lay on me. After a while, I got up and went upstairs to find Dad; he was standing in the hallway. The light was very dim, and I could not see him very well. I tried to turn on the light, but it will not come on, and so I continued to walk toward him.

As I approached him, he was different. He started to talk about other things, like men did thousands of years ago, and for some reason I began to cry, and I felt a sense of loneliness as I reached out to him. He received me, but almost immediately I got the feeling that I should not be hugging him, and it was because of what I remembered years ago. I had been picked up, turned upside down, and carried into a room with no doors or windows. Then I was laid face down in a straightway position and was later told to rise. This man felt like that man.

This man, the one who only looked like my father, lifted me up on my back and carried me through the wall into a house and into a room where I picked up some nails that were on a table.

4:05 a.m.   I Am Taken to Hell to Face Him but It's Not Our Time Yet

(b) I was in my room; I felt the air stirring, and I got that feeling that something was about to happen. On the table were some nails, and then I had them in my hand. I was taken face down through the floor and then through a concrete wall and a distance in darkness that I could not see through. I was taken before my father. I stood and he knelt before me as I began to say words over him. I still had the nails in my hand. I was lifted up, and taken in a laying position, face up, all the way around the room, close to the walls, corner to corner.

I was outside the concrete wall, looking at the corner of the concrete wall, and thinking I was going to be rammed into that corner edge as I was once before, but this time I was taken backward, face up, down toward the ground. I was taken down into the earth fast, and I saw nothing as I looked up and around me. We traveled a long time until I came to what is known as hell to some. I saw at a distance one man, and I watched him as he caused pain and made two other men do terrible things to each other. I called out to all of them, "Stop." They all noticed me, but he alone was the one to end this—this was his place. We started to fight, and as we fought, he still tried to kill the other man by placing a knife where the man had no choice but to fall on it when he pulled him down. I continued to fight to prevent it, but the vision was over, and I was back in my room. In my hand were the nails, three of them different sizes, and I put them back on the table.

The nails represent what I will face for challenging the way the world has evolved, and the darkness it has built over life itself and its beliefs. Taken face down and through a concrete wall is giving me authority to face what is before me—an impenetrable wall or divider that none can pass through unless carried or elevated to a certain position by the Father///.

Him, the one I will face, is the one who represents the rule of order that cannot be broken but is broken by him or those who rule in his name willingly or unknowingly.

08/30/97   5:16 a.m.   A Young Lady Cries Sitting in a Fire

My daughter and I were in the Del Ray section of Alexandria. We went out there on a bus just to walk around and see what was going on because the place had gotten so large and spread out. We walked for a while and then got on what I thought was going to be a bus, but it turned out to be a horse-drawn carriage. We got on and another couple joined us. The carriage took off, and after a short time, the other couple and my daughter got off, and my daughter said, "I am going to buy something." The carriage then had only a young lady, the driver, and me, and after riding around for a while, the young lady and I got out of the carriage. The place seemed like New Orleans, Louisiana. I followed the young woman with the short hair, and she seemed to know where she was going and said we could catch the carriage later.

She walked out in front of me on the path we were walking down, and I ended up pretty far behind. I saw her fall down, and I began to holler for help. When I got close to her, I could see she fell into a wood-burning fire that must have been set earlier by someone on the path; I ran to her quickly to help her up. When I got to her, I saw a young woman I did not know. She was crying holding her arm that had caught on fire, but she was still sitting in the blazing fire. I wondered why she cried about her arm while she was still sitting in the fire, and then she turned back into the young woman I had followed from the carriage. I saw two women: the first I did not know and the second I knew. She was one person and then the other. She then looked at me and said, "I threw her in the fire," and I watched her change again. I had just gotten her up out of the fire, and she ran off down the path a short distance. She looked back at me, and I saw the young woman I knew earlier again. I ran and caught her and put my hands on the front and back of her head, and I held her as I began to pray out very loud—so loud that others turned to see us. I did not know what they thought, but I did not stop, and the two began to separate, to become two separate young women. As they became two separate beings, I continued to pray, and the new one began to dissolve into liquid on the ground. When all that was left was a spot on the ground, I blew my breath on it and blew it away from us. The other young woman I let go, and she cried out that I was a dirty old man.

09/22/97   8:54 a.m.   Oil Spill—Tropical Plants and Catfish All Covered with Oil

I was looking at a black fish. I think it was a catfish with oil all over it. I looked at the place where this fish was laying; it was in the center of our tropical plants. Our plants were under the covering that this fish was laying on. As I got closer, I saw another fish much larger than the catfish; but it was not a fish, it was an otter or something like that, and it was covered with black stuff too. I saw tails and legs; it was two otters. As I looked at the plants along the edge, I saw many other things were covered with something. I just wanted to find clean water for that fish. I remove some plants to better care for them, and that's when I saw more otters, all dead and covered in black oil. I continued to work.

I believe this turned out to be the gulf oil spill off our coastline in 2010.

Book XI

10/13/97　2:40 a.m.　Atlantis Continues

I was in an area where the law was from another world. I had come here with beings from another world, and I worked with them, but they treated the humans here different, sometimes very bad. Then a time came when I had to battle my own kind, and we ended up turning it over to the humans to run again. I talked to the humans for the last time here, and I told them I would leave for a place on the east coast of America and from there I would find my way home. My kind would pick me up there. All the others of my kind were gone.

10/22/97　6:00 a.m.　The Dream That Saved a Sailor's Life

I was a sailor. I sailed the seas all around the world, but mostly I sailed in the Pacific realm, where I trusted my feelings to tell me when and where I should sail. I had traveled with a lot of captains on their ships, but one certain trip could have been my last. It all started months before I met this new captain. I had one of those dreams where I saw myself on a ship, hiding in a small room, a room I stayed in and did not come out of for fear of my life.

It was months later that I met this new captain; I had only seen a couple of female captains before. She fell in love with me as soon as she saw me, and I with her. She was a hard-drinking woman, and her love for me never stopped, but one night when the ship was in port, I had that same dream about being in a small room again, and it scared me badly. I seemed to be very afraid of whatever was outside that room, as I was too scared to come out, but this dream told me why I was in the small room. We were on the high seas, and everyone's hand was on a rig watching the sails, because we were about to go into "change-over water," water where you could go from fifty to one hundred feet deep to thousands of feet deep. The place was the Marianas, where you could be shallow water for twenty or thirty miles then it got too deep to measure. It was there I saw a monster with many arms; it held our ship still until it tore down our sails, and it ate men like I eat meat. I ran into the small room, and the captain came behind me, calling me, but I would not answer her or anyone, and I stayed in that small room in the dark. I did not move or make any noise at all, but I heard troubling noises all around. Then I woke up and decided from those dreams that I would not sail with this female captain on that day or any other day.

Many months later, I heard her ship was lost at sea with all hands, and I always thought I knew what did it, and I thought that the dreams saved me.

11/30/97   8:48 a.m.   I Witnessed This: a Chair of Earth Would Be the Seat of Water

I witnessed a father tell his son to dig out a chair that sat outside within a mound of dirt on a small rise. It looked like a chair, but the seat area was only earth. It had to have the earth removed until a man could stand up inside it. The son dug out the chair and removed the earth, and it was finished. The son and the father left, and I looked at the chair and it was not finished; it could not hold water at this point. There was dirt where the arms of the chair should have been, so I began to brush the area where the arms were supposed to be until it was ready to hold water. A chair was formed, and its seat would be a seat of water. I continued to work so the father would not know it was not finished.

The son removed the earth just enough for man to start understanding the power to be free in self-belief. Now they need to see their actual faiths really work, not ideology, but an overall understanding that really works—that all can share in as they please.

12/08/97   2:35 a.m.   Flying, Spinning like a Drill

We were all out in a park with a large bay on one side and a river on the other; we were having fun and then it happened. I began to turn around like a drill bit, spinning faster and faster. I was up off the ground, turning like a spinning top, and moving so fast that I could cut down trees better than a machine. After a while, I began to fly fast all over the place—here and there in seconds—and then I got close to the power lines, but they did not burn or shock me as I expected them to. I did have a problem though; I could not get away from the power lines, and when I finally did, I fell to the earth with no power. Then I felt a small surge of power kick in from the Father///, and this all made me think, "Did I do something wrong before that made me lose my power?"

12/18/97   6:46 a.m.   A Templar Takes His Corner

I was a member of this church, and I worked in the administration of the church. We opened the church, and everyone walked in and took their seats, except for a few who had other jobs to do. The pastor called a member, he called him a Templar, and he had to walk fast from one corner of the church to the other. Different Templar's took various corners. I saw two, one ran from one corner to the other, and then another ran from the next corner to the other corner, guarding it for a length of time.

I sat there looking around this new room; it had been on my mind for some time to try to get into this room and to be able to pray here, but it was too late then as the others were there. I knew all of them very well, as we all worked together, and then I heard some talk about the Masonic order, but I was not sure if it was here or earlier.

01/04/98   6:31 a.m.   My Father/// Guides Me on My Path, Shows Me Every Step

I was shown and taught my path very slowly—shown all the steps I had to take. I was shown everything twice, preparing to be able to do it all on my own. The beginning of the path I was shown: when to do it, where to do it, and how to do it. I was older now, and it had started to happen.

I began to run the course, up and down the stairs, through places with all types of people looking at me. I first began to climb all the stairs one step at a time, and then two at a time, meeting people coming down. None were going my way at that time. At the top, I met a man, tall and thin, and I told him something about my father's size in a joking manner, as if the man standing before was not my father, but he was. I did not know him very well looking at him, and I saw him only after the course was over and after the last steps were made—as I went through the door and closed it. He stood right inside the area of the door, not on my course at all but in the room. He had talked me through this course many times before. But when I ran the course the last time, I seemed to be on my own.

From my childhood, I was shown first who was with me and how it would help me on my path, and it taught me what my actions should be toward others. I began to see visions at a young age; some were the type you could not forget, and I did not want to forget them. During all this and through my teen years, I was alone physically and no one knew except my mother. The man who talked me through the course was the one in the room with no windows or doors—that within us.

01/10/98   3:41 a.m.   I Get Vibrations inside a Golden Elevator

I got into an elevator behind one other person, and as the door closed, this person faded back into the corner of the elevator until he was gone. All I saw were a few black ashes floating around me. Then I got vibrations as if I was going to be taken through physical objects, except this time I just stood there looking at the door and walls of this golden elevator. I somehow lost a little time while standing there, but I came back to the present. All this happened inside the golden elevator, and the elevator itself had never moved at all.

01/13/98   10:25 a.m.   If I Cannot Finish My Duty, OneOther Will Finish It

(a) I was at home in the bed, dreaming about my daughter, and I got up because my brother was in the house, and I had something to tell him. Before I could tell him, we began to argue until it got heated about who the boss was and who should run things. The argument got worse because he wanted to run things his way, and I said no, it had to be done my way, and if anything happened to me, he could take over and complete it. I said, "I trust you with all I have, but until then I will run things." After all of that, I felt guilty, and I needed something and did not know what.

My brother in this vision is OneOther, but in life we must do it together because he knows all the things I do not, and he knows what's in front of me.

A Force Greater than a Hurricane Ranges over Water

(b) There was a force so large, so powerful, and it ranged over water mostly, and I stayed away from it. The one with me, OneOther, seemed not to be afraid; he even rode a vehicle out in front of the force, and it went through and over him. It seemed to be visible and invisible at the same time, and maybe the water gave it shape. I saw it moving with the power of a hurricane—or something larger.

01/24/98   I Drew a Triangle in the Dirt with a Circle Around It

I was with two friends, crossing the school field fast, heading to our special place. As we arrived, I started to draw in the dirt, a circle and then a triangle, but we each had to take a corner, and we did not have enough people to do that. We were waiting on one more person, but I needed him now. One of the guys said, "You had better hurry up," as if we were doing something wrong or time was running out. There were three of us, and I thought about using one of the school kids—who was not far off and was looking at us—to stand on one corner. If having someone stand on the fourth corner was a problem, I could counter it by using a double circle instead of a single one.

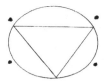

01/25/98   6:44 a.m.   A Universal Timepiece Made of Cellular Material

I saw a timepiece, a human gage of some kind, that represented man's sense and his or her ability over mechanical things, but it was much more special than that. All these were timepieces or small clocks of some kind, and they were all part of men and women in some way. It was like every single thing was calculated to its finest point, as if every single thing had its time and they were all counting down together—or counting up, I am not sure which. All were connected to the universal timepiece or schedule.

This vision tells the whole story of the Atlantean bloodline. The timepiece above is a human cell, but could it represent all living cells and their evolutionary schedules as we move into the next human upgrade. It tells me we are on a schedule not made or controlled by us, a schedule that will keep its own time for all things.

9:38 a.m. People from New York Came to Look at Warehouse Space

(a) A group of people had come from New York to look at available warehouse space for storage of caskets.

A Prisoner Under Lock and Key Gets Away

(b) I walked into a room where an officer was in charge of keeping a prisoner. I look at this officer, and he looked too scared to stop anybody, so I decide to help him. I took his gun, a .45 caliber automatic. Immediately I saw how big the gun was, but now it was my duty to watch the prisoner. The prisoner got up and just decided to go, so I raised my weapon and pointed it at him. But the gun was heavy. I noticed I had to have it up near my chin and mouth. It would just hit me if I pulled the trigger; I would cause that gun to kick me in the face. Then I did not see the prisoner, and I had to get him back, but he was a big guy.

A Man Comes Back from New York Looking at Storage Space Again

(c) One man had come down from New York and wanted to look at the same warehouse space, again to store caskets in. He looked at the warehouse space but went through to the outside and looked at that too as we talked to him. The man told us he had to make sure this was a good location.

The three visions would soon make sense to me, but not until 2010 when an old sailing ship was discovered under the wreckage of the twin towers in New York.

01/27/98 5:06 a.m. Airborne Soldiers Jump into Germany During World War II

I was in school, jump-school training at the army's airborne training center—infantry airborne they called it—and there were a lot of young guys here. They were showing us pictures and movies of planes dropping bombs on trains and train yards in Germany.

I had just arrived from infantry boot camp, and I seemed to like it so far, but tomorrow they were going to have us go up in a plane to get an idea of the height of our jumps for the first time. I was joking with somebody about the fact that this would not be my first jump, as I had fallen off the bunk bed this morning, and the joke did not go over so well with the others.

02/05/98 6:38 a.m. A Sea Captain from an Old Sailing Ship Just Appears

I was in the back of some warehouses. I began to see movement in a certain area—in a funny way it was like a cube of space, and it moved funny. It moved differently than the surrounding space did, and as I looked, I saw an old man walk through from some place. I moved to get a better look, and he was looking in my direction. I saw that he looked like an old sea captain on one of the old sailing ships. When he looked at me, he started to move faster, away from me for some reason.

Later, I heard him talking to another member of his crew saying, "I never served him as king," and he was crying. He had seen someone who looked like a king from his past, and he was hurt and worried.

I had two visions in the above January 25, 1998, vision, and I did not know what to do with them, but in 2010, at the site of the World Trade Center, an old sailing vessel was found. The old sailing vessel was under that site, and it connected the two visions for me and actually made it mean something.

02/14/98   2:03 a.m.   Flying Objects Made of Crystal

I was in my bedroom. I got up and went into the bathroom; I saw something lying near the floor, and I bent down to get it and the light went dim. I stood up and flipped the light switch, but it did nothing. As I turned to leave, something started to happen, and it scared me. I had on my bathrobe, and it felt like magnetism: something was pulling my whole body and everything back into the bathroom. I got out of the door, but my bathrobe and the tie on it were being pulled straight back inside the bathroom.

When I finally got clear of the door, I felt as if I was going to be taken away. I looked out my front door and there were three costumed figures, full of something within them. They looked like stuffed animals except one was a hairy man, one was a funny clown, and one was something I could not figure out at all. The figures were hung up, and I wanted them down, but I was lifted and taken through the wall outside, right by those stuffed things. I thought that what lifted me was going to let me take those stuffed figures down, but then I saw that the stuffed figures outside my window were still hanging there and something was still holding me.

I was then carried south, up high through a large city. Then it got much higher and I saw all kinds of flying objects in the sky, and most were made of crystal. They were all shapes of crystal, and you could see through them. All of them were made like some type of aircraft. I saw a couple of planes that look like our most advanced planes but made of crystal like the rest—even though they looked like ours, they were different. Two interstellar craft had come down right by my left shoulder, but they were metal looking. They landed at an airport, but it was different from the kind we have. The sky was filled with all sizes and shapes of these craft, and some formed shapes of objects like star groups.

I was a little worried. I felt as if I could fall, and it was the first time for this. My right hand held onto what could only be called a thumb, and I could not tell what my left hand held onto. My feet felt as if they were at the edge of what I was standing on.

I was taken to a large river, and as I looked at it, I was told I could have it all, and all I had to do was follow instructions and do what I was told. I did not have any problem with that. All the time I faced forward, and the river was now behind me. I also saw buildings taller than any I ever saw, which manufactured bicycles, beach balls, and beach supplies of all kinds. When the other buildings stopped going up, this structure was still growing. I began to think about the words, "Obey and follow instructions," so I turned slowly to face that which carried me from behind, and it was a beautiful brown-skinned women, with short hair in the style that I like. I embraced her and kissed her, and I knew I could handle it; I could just say no to her if I needed to at any time.

3:58 p.m.   The Same White Bearded Sea Capitan Says
                I Know Who He Is

I was at my home at North West Street, and I was thinking about an old sea captain who visited us earlier. I did not know him, but I had met or seen him a few times. I started to walk around the house picking up keys, single keys, keys in pairs, and bunches of them that were just lying around everywhere. I put them in a glass container on the coffee table.

I went upstairs to the bathroom, and I heard someone coming in downstairs. I turned around and went back down the stairs to the living room, and I saw the old sea captain. I said, "Who are you?" and he sat down and put his leg across another chair, saying nothing. He was white and had a white beard, and he was in his sixties or seventies, I guessed. I continue to ask him the same thing until he said, "You know who I am." That was when I recognized the voice. It was him, at least the voice was. I said, "Okay, it's you, but it's not you—you are the same but not the same."

02/21/98   4:38 a.m.   Thirty Days I Saw It, Thirty Days It Happened

I was in Warrenton, Virginia, where I was born. I was with two friends who were Native American, and we stood around a table talking and looking at a table full of different kinds of food. One of our friends had come over with an a adjustable wrench, and he put it up close to my neck and acted as if he was adjusting or straightening something in my neck. When he was finished I asked them to wait while I went to another house and got my book that I wanted him to see.

When I returned I showed them in my book a picture of a man who was standing beside another man holding a tool of some kind around his neck, just as he had done to mine. I showed him the date—it was exactly thirty days before from the present day. He looked at it, but he was caught by another picture in the book, a picture of a mountain range that I had drawn. He took a picture out of his pocket, and he took my book and showed them to our friend who with us, the pictures matched. I told them, "I don't know what you are talking about, but you had better do something quick because there is natural gas and oil on the property." I told them that what I drew was in the future, but they had better act now before someone else did.

8:33 a.m.   A Holy Man from Tibet Will Tell Me My Future

I was told that a holy man from Tibet, near or in China, would give me the front side of my path, and that the backside would be mine to find out.

03/02/98   6:41 a.m.   El-Amin Saved Me So I Could See the Light Again

I was in a small office building working on a light that was battery operated. I took it apart and separated the main sections to test them. El-Amin had come in and covered one of the parts so I could not see it. It made me so mad that I called him a dirty name. I could not ever remember calling anyone a name like that, and right as I did it, just that quick, all of the lights in the building went dim and all sound stopped. The sounds of so many people doing different things and the noise of equipment, all of it stopped for me and became completely silent. Then, in the darkness, El-Amin touched my forehead and made the sign of the cross on it. I did not know what had happened, but after he did that the light came up and the sounds came back. I must have done something to him that was so wrong that I immediately lost everything, and his touch, faith, and forgiveness freed me.

03/21/98   5:16 a.m.   Gangs, Groups, Killing Each Other, They Had to Find a Way to Stop

I was looking at gang members and groups of boys and girls not necessarily in gangs but in trouble. We were all at a meeting, and they had come on buses and anything they could to be there. This was the first meeting; the second one was almost stopped before it got started—by outsiders trying to help. Killing each other daily, they wanted to give themselves a chance, and we were all there for that reason. I remembered walking into the third meeting, and everyone was seated, and the place was sparkling, with a disco atmosphere. I walked about halfway through the room, and I started to smile at what I saw. The man who was the disc jockey started a record or CD, and it took the longest time to get the cymbals and drums going. I never got a chance to speak.

03/24/98   12:24 a.m.   Lifted and Pulled at Great Speeds and Then Taken through Many Walls

I went to bed, and I felt myself go off to sleep. I was pulled out of the bed and taken through walls at incredible speeds. I thought to relax as I went through many buildings with different wall thicknesses: concrete, steel, tin, brick, and drywall. I traveled a very long way and saw many things. I entered a dark area that I thought was Africa because I saw baboons and monkeys, and their footprints were on the ground everywhere. We flew so far so fast, and all the time hands held me. I felt the hands that held me, and to my left I saw a little of the clothing worn by the one carrying me. It was light green and light orange, one cloth over the other, and worn down to the feet, which I did not see.

I did not try to see more than I was given privilege to see, and as I was taken inside a very large building, I saw all the monkeys, cats, and other small animals that were in cages there. Even inside this building, I was up very high. The hands that carried me were taken off gently, and I flew on my own. I continued at speed, but when I tried to go throw a tin wall, I could not. I only spun like a drill bit at thousands of revolutions per second, yet I saw everything as if I were not spinning at all. I said spinning, because when my head hit the tin wall, I could hear my head cutting it like an electric blade, yet neither of us, the wall or I, gave in. I finally gave up and decided to stay in the building, where I figured I was given the privilege to fly.

I will be given the opportunity to go and see many things, and at no time will I be alone in what I will do or where I will go. The most important thing is, like the animals in the cage, I am not ready to come out yet, and it will be easier for me if I learn this quickly. Like on my grandfather's place, I have an area and a time in which to work.

04/08/98   5:54 a.m.   It Came to Me What the Vision
                              Meant—Eddie Murphy

I was looking at a scene like in a play; one man was standing on a mountain (Eddie Murphy, the actor), and he had a rifle in his hand. Below him were three or four men and thousands of guns on the ground everywhere—as if a battle had been lost.

I was in bed thinking about the vision I just had when I heard the door open. It was Dad, and he was headed into the other room. It had come to me what the vision really meant, and I rushed in the room where Dad was, and I said, "You haven't done anything with a gun lately, have you?" He was in the closet, and he turned around with a double-barrel shotgun in his hands. I said to him as he walked past me, "Don't lend him your gun; he will never give it back to you," and Dad half-smiled at me while walking out of the front door.

Dad had just left when a young man walked in with some papers for us. I looked at them, and it was information on our stock plan. It showed our dividend for the period was forty dollars—not much of a return.

[I woke up to write this down and it hit me: it was not "stock return money." It was a key to decipher the vision. It was not a small return, but soon it would be a large one—and it was not money either. Eddie Murphy was normally the hero but not this time. One man has saved a nation, but never has one man moved a world away from war to the beginnings of peace.

One man can stop the battle, and one man can stop the battles he controls, but he must understand there are those who will not want to stop because of reasons of their own, and that's the three or four looking up at the man on the mountain as he wonders what has happened to all the others. Some seem as if they never want to stop the battle or war.

04/09/98   12:04 a.m.   OneOther Said "Is That You?" and I Said, "Yes"

I was in my repair shop with OneOther working on a pneumatic control for a hydraulic jack; it was an air-over hydraulic system for a floor jack. I worked as he talked to me. I had to get a new repair kit, and as I opened it, he said, "Ed, is that you? You know what I mean." And I said, "Yes, it is me," but something grabbed me. It had a hold of me, and I started to pray to the Father/// like always, but this time I understood

89

what kept it from working years ago. I was still praying, saying, "Father///, thank you for all things, for all things are yours in nature, seen and unseen, and we are yours." Then what held me, kissed me, and I kissed it back, and it released me.

04/12/98   7:10 a.m.   OneOther, a Young Lady, and I Are Looking at Two Granite Crypts

I was in Warrenton, Virginia, with a young lady who I believed was my intended, and we were on my uncle Aaron's property, not far from the Warrenton bypass, looking at two granite crypts. One of the crypts was a sand color, and it was the one I was being shown. A lady was buried in it, and I was to open it and discover its contents. The tall thin young lady with me said, "You must wait a while longer," and she showed me another piece of marble granite and said, "The one you are to open is not ready yet." I see the two colors are not exact, but one is not fully cured yet.

As I stood at our door, I saw under the door something ease its head in. I first thought of a snake, but I quickly saw that it was carpentry or mechanics tools. The first piece was a ruler, and before I could say, "I need that," it jumped into my hands. Then two other pieces entered, but they stayed on the floor. I said to the young lady with me that I wanted to use the ruler, and eighteen inches of the rule stretched out and stuck up above my hand. As I said or asked that question, it bent to the right fast and back to position; quickly, I asked a question about the crypt, and again it said okay by bending to the right. I was told that in less than thirty days I could open the crypt.

I turned to my sweetheart and kissed her a long kiss, and when it was over, I had some kind of glue or stain on my entire tongue that I did not know how to get off. Others around me went on with what they were doing, but I just stood there with a waxed tongue.

04/16/98   6:47 a.m.   Novak Columnist and the Senate Ethics Panel

I was down on the river fishing, and lots of people were around. I saw everything in the water: people, boats, all kinds of things. I also saw an alligator attack a young man on the river, it happened twice, but they did not stop getting in the water.

Then I saw a woman, whose name I knew was Sarah. She was standing there with eight envelopes in her hand that had names on them like "Novak," "Ethics Senate Panel," and other departments. I was standing there as she came up to me. We talked. She needed to see the president, Bill Clinton, about an issue. I talked with her and then began to laugh out loud, because at that very moment the president—Bill, as he was known to me—was walking up the adjacent sidewalk. He probably wanted to know what I was laughing about, but he continued by with his protection detail around him. I thought someone else could probably help us first, since Sarah was there with eight interoffice envelopes, and I knew Bob Novak.

04/17/98   2:42 a.m.   What Is an Enigma

I was asked a simple question, "What is an enigma," and that is all the voice said.

My answer now is "Something very hard to figure out, if at all: me."

04/25/98   12:17 a.m.   Statues of Monks in Vietnam

I was riding in an airplane, thinking about Vietnam. I was in one part of the country and thinking about another part of country that I saw on the flight. I was looking at a coastline as the plane went in very low. There were lots of mountains all along the coast, and I begin to see statues of monks. The plane took us up the mountain, and I saw statue after statue. After six or seven, I saw a person at the next statue, and at each statue after that I saw a person. Then at the next three statues, I saw more than one person at a time, which made me wish I had counted all the statues to this point. This was very beautiful country.

04/26/98   9:44 a.m.   The Light in Front of the Ark of the
                            Covenant Shows the Way

I was at home with my family when the door-to-door salesperson, who brought us orange juice and other things we liked, came by. He always looked at a large vase we had and how it was shaped. It had no bottom because a second vase would be put inside it for light, which burned by oil. He was interested because it was like the light that was carried before the ark to show or guide the way, and it had a way of burning bright or dim depending on the right or wrong direction, and it burned all the time. The first vase was open on both ends, and the second one was sealed just for us. One salesperson, who was Jewish, brought two more, and we all looked at them. This one salesperson always had to use the bathroom, and he made a loud noise every time.

05/05/98   3:31 a.m.   Celebration and Prayer from a Native American Father

We were driving along in our car, a family looking at all the sights, when we saw a large shopping center with a large celebration of some kind going on. I saw many Native Americans. My father decided to stop, and we got out and walked around and had a chance to see all the sights before getting back on the road again.

A Native American father with many years gone by said, "Father///, I thank you for so many years upon the earth, years as many and as full as the buffalo in old times. I now see many of my own children grown and may see them this day for the last time. For today, I have refused to stay home and not be a part of this great day of celebration. I have seen so many moons pass, and I have seen the great iron horse that trespassed on our lands and our children who grew and cut their hair in the new ways of the soulless ones. My years, my time upon the earth, I do not know, but I have seen much, and I am very tired. My people celebrated the coming of a new age. The new age and new ways from one who will lead us back to the old ways—when the Great Spirit led us from hunting ground to hunting ground, and our own lodges were as many as the buffalo."

The daughter of this wise old one said, "Father, you must rest now, and if you do not rest you will not be able to see all the wonderful things going on." She called some of the family members to help move him where she pointed, but he said, "No, leave me here, daughter."

A boy and his family were walking around and looking at the many people standing around this very old Native American chief and medicine man—there must have been hundreds or even thousands of people there looking, listening for anything he might say. It was told over the generations that he had led his people with his dreams, and he always slept to get the answers.

Then the old father said, "Daughter." And she replied, "Yes, Father." He said, "I feel for the first time in a long journey that I must lead the people in a song," and he began to sing, lying in my bed. He sang about the new day, and the new way that was sister to the old way, and that he had made it to see this great day start. He sang about the goodness of the Father/// and his leadership through all things. He sang about how many of them were black as midnight to red as the sands at the foot of their mountains.

Then he said, "Like all of us, I had everything taken from me, but it shall all be given back. Many lose, but a few win, and the one who leads those who now seek a soul shall receive justly for what they have given." He prayed as loud as he could, saying, "I pray unto you, Father///. I open my arms, and I run to you my Father///, to be in your arms. I wait on your call to see all your glory when you call for me."

The young woman could only look on as her father sang. She felt it would be his last. He had sung for his people throughout his years, and I grew up listening to him. I grew up with a father who was a father to all earth tribes, and now this might be his last day. He only wanted to see the child who was supposed to come and lead all people as one. I did not want him to make the trip, but he did what he wanted to do, so we had moved his bed from his home here. He sang his song, and all the people listened to him. People from everywhere came here to celebrate this day and week. He is my great-grandfather five times over. I saw him lift his arms up to the sky dwellers as though he wanted to go with them, and then they came down to his side as he just stared. I rushed to his side and felt him, and he was gone. And I said, "Good-bye, Father."

"Daddy, can you buy me a soda?"

"Come on, we are a long way from home out here, down here, where ever we are. Get in the car, it is time to go."

5:30 a.m.   The Four Silent Ones Come Forth

I was told to come to a hospital. It was a military installation, and when I got there I went to the rear entrance, but it was closed. I had been there before, and I saw a door was open, but two attendants sat in front of it, and I would not go in that way. That was when I started to think about going around to the front entrance. But I did not; I just waited.

It got dark, and I decided to go around to the front anyway, but as I did I saw a creature with hoofed feet and hair all over its body, and I knew he wanted me. I moved back into the shadows, out of sight, as it passed me and went to the back gate. All I could see was a figure, not the actual being. It came my way and I was very quiet, because it could hear anything, and even see my heat trace. It came right at me; I didn't move, but it got me, and as it grabbed me, it did so in an easy manner, and I felt something different. It was not trying to hurt me at all, and as I talked to it, it carried me to the front entrance of the hospital. I also saw it was not hoofed at all. That's when I saw the others, all a little taller than me, the Four Silent Ones.

As I watched them, the Four Silent Ones said something together and began to grow and become the colors of the earth—a hundred feet high. They began to call on the one who I must face, that wanted to hurt me, and said, "Come and do battle."

As all this was happening, I lay in bed in a hospital room. A nurse came in, took a needle, took the end cap off, and tried to stick me with it. I wrestled with her and finally got it, and she got another one from her pocketbook and tried it again. She did this five or six times, and finally I got her pocketbook and dumped it out on the floor. She started to cry, looking at me, and said, "Why did you do that? I must get this done."

05/10/98   8:47 a.m.   The Life of a Young Woman and Two Ways It Could Turn Out

I was walking with a friend when he asked me if I saw a particular play. I said no, but when we reached the place where the play was to take place, I recognized the rooms. It was my home. I watched the play, and it was as if I had seen something like it before in my past.

I saw the complete life of a young woman growing up as a person, the influences that would shape her, and the outcomes of each. I saw the two ways it could turn out and saw that we had the power to change the outcome. If it could not be done as before, everyone would have to take a part in making the change.

A course was set, and the question was, should that course and our thinking be changed? This was a big problem for the Four Silent Ones who saw things take place and took no part. At the end of the play, everyone came out front and bowed before the audience. I saw people from all walks of life, including a nun dressed in black and white, taking part in this play. You could not just preach a system, you had to live the system, and we did have a choice.

The young lady has been taught the difference between right and wrong, not "my" idea of right and wrong, but the Ten Commandments—a lot of us are trying to live by that. The Four Silent Ones are the four angels that stand on the four corners of the earth. We still have the time, but are we willing to make the change? Or will we continue this path to possible destruction?

9:36 a.m.   People Think Everything Will Be Okay the Way It Is

I saw scenes of people living in different parts of our country and everyone seemed okay. I heard them say, "Everything will be okay the way it is." They seemed to think that things would change on their own and that nothing needed to be done for that to happen. It seemed to me that all of them were dressed wrong for the different parts of the country they now lived in. Where they lived and what they were wearing did not match.

05/16/98   4:44 a.m.   A House of a Former Slave Owner Is Full of Souls

We lived in a very large house and had lots of guests. We had just settled down for the evening in the large living room where I had a daybed. We had just started to talk when a doctor entered the room from somewhere, talking in his usual manner—to himself or someone even though he was alone.

The house was the size of a mansion on an estate of many, many acres; it was built in the early 1700s and had many slaves. Two types of beings lived there now, those that were alive and those that were dead but had not yet passed on for some reason. One of the residents was a man who grew to hate everyone around him during the days of slavery, including his family for some reason. He had owned the house.

I owned the house now. We all sat in the living room, and I was lying on the daybed as the doctor came in. I guessed right away that he had been in the wine cellar—he looked like it. I said to him, "Where have you been?" And he said, "Just reading." He had a big thick book with five or six thousands pages to it. He stood there with his book, and I said, "I guess you have been in the wine cellar." "Oh no, I have not," he said, and just then a few pages in his book flipped over on their own. I said, "I knew it—you are lying. One of the many souls in the house, probably one of the children, let me know by doing that." He got mad and began to talk about someone accusing him of wrongdoing, and he handed the book to the young woman with him, who could hardly carry it. Before this young woman could take a step, it seemed that all the pages of the book, every single sheet, turned over by itself while she held it. When it stopped, she left the room, and the doctor left behind her.

Two of us were resting in the large daybed, when all of a sudden, we were pulled by our ankles off the daybed onto the floor and laid opposite the daybed—why, I was not sure. We lay there until it was over. Then we got up. When those things happened we did not do anything or say anything; it would happen, and it would stop with no problem. After we got up, I walked with Dad for a while, and then he called for one of the young ladies who worked there, and he walked off to find her.

As I passed one of the rooms off the living room, I saw a shadow and I looked closer. It was the young lady Dad was looking for. She was sleeping under the stairs off the hallway. Where she was, she could not be seen unless you knew where to look. I said nothing, and I walked over to where she was. She was under some clothes, laying there naked. She looked so beautiful, brown, and full of life, and as I stood there, she woke up. She got up and began putting her things on very fast. Her father saw us and called her. Then I heard a loud cry from one of the other women who worked there in the house.

I rushed to see what was wrong, and I heard her say, "The doctor is dead" and that he had been almost smashed flat by the wine press, a big vat in the cellar. I said, "I know who did this," and I called out, "Old man, come out here now." Again I called out, "Old man, come out here," and he came out. I saw a young lady of his run out of the room, and I called him again, "Come out here now, I say," and then he came out looking for the girl.

Now no one could see their spirit forms except me, and you hardly ever saw the old man. He came out walking fast, trying to catch up to his daughter who was seventeen or eighteen years old, and he walked right past me. I called out to him again, "You hear me, old man." It was the only name I knew to call him. I went a few feet and grabbed his coat. He looked like Ben Franklin. I turned him, and even then he would not look at me. I did not act scared, but I did not really know what he might do. I accused him of killing the doctor, and he said nothing. So I got right up into his face as much as I could. He was a very tall man and was dressed in his black suit with the big lapels. I kept telling him that he had killed the doctor, and he turned his head side to side. I began to pray, and I ended up telling him how much I cared about him and all the others in the house. I told him that I cared about them not being able move on or cross over, and right before me he began to get younger, from sixties or seventy to maybe thirty. I kept talking to him until I woke up, saying, "I forgive you and love you."

6:32 a.m.   We Performed the Circle of Prayer for Someone

I was in a class with other students, both older and younger, when I was asked to bless the food. I walked up front and stood before the class, and I began to pray "Our Father///, which art in Heaven" and so on until I was finished with the prayer. Then I asked if there were any requests for prayer, and I heard something, but with all the others talking I did not know where it came from. I saw my friend Carolyn sitting in a chair to my right, and in front of me sat a light-skinned woman about sixty years old who was talking, and I said to her, "Be quiet, please." And I called again for whoever might want a special prayer. I heard a voice of a friend of mine saying, "He has one." It was a young man. I said, "Do you want a special prayer or not?" He got up fast and came toward me. I told those there to form a circle and join hands with the young man and me in the center. The women I told to be quiet earlier said, "You have to have a gift to give the Father/// for him to come," and I said, "Please be quiet and hold hands." She kept saying the same thing, and I kept saying to her to be quiet, and finally I said, "I pray and I pray only to the Father/// and nothing else," and she finally got quiet, and I turned back to the young man to start.

05/21/98   3:54 a.m.   He Carried the "John the Conqueror Root" with Him Everywhere

My partner and I were in an outlying town where the law was a man who used black magic and witchcraft and carried a large root called a John the Conquer root around with him. He had followers so tied up in magic that they could not see anything else. On this day, with other law enforcement agencies, we were going to try to take his organization down. When we arrived at his well-known place, he was gone and there was no evidence at all that he was ever there. He always seemed to get all the information on whatever was happening before we could get there to make an arrest.

When we did finally catch him and some of his group, we went through everything we could find and came up with nothing. This was not his main business place, so we let him go, but he knew we were onto him and that made it harder. A few days later, we found a person who told us about his hold on people and where he kept his power source over them. We followed this voodoo worker as he went to his car, and we followed as he drove to a building and went in. When he came out, he put something in his trunk. We thought it was what we were looking for—without that, he would feel powerless.

We waited for night, laying alongside a house in a ditch, when, to our left, came twenty or thirty people who could not see us. These people knew he did not have the power then, and they had planned to take matters into their own hands. We heard the noise and saw them attack him. We joined in at the right time, then we got to his car. It was surrounded by garbage and dead animal parts everywhere. We opened the trunk to get the root. They would take him in, the US Marshals Service that led this joint operation.

05/26/98   9:32 a.m.   Ancient Tomb—a Black Gemstone Marks
Its Location

I was told about a black stone, and I saw it in an ancient tomb, buried by the remains of someone—a black stone embedded in the wall. This stone was the starting point for finding the missing parts that connected everything together.

06/14/98   9:13 a.m.   First There Were Three and Then I
Became Part of the Three

It took three, three things to make the change. At first, he had made the change using the three, and now I would make the same kind of change, but I removed the one and added myself to make the three. First, he was part of the three, and then I was part of the three.

Book XII

06/28/98   6:14 p.m.   The Ark of the Covenant/// and My Hair
on a Tray

    I had in my hands the container that the ark of the covenant was kept in, but there was no covenant, no written paper within the container. I was standing on a football field by my school. I had bills to pay, and in front of me was a small tray that I held that had a piece of my hair on it. I was looking at my hair on the tray as if it were money or a way to pay something. I remember being told and shown what had happened to the contents of the container.

08/05/98   8:20 a.m.   Left and Right Hand

08/16/98   4:53 a.m.   Right Hand Backside

08/25/98   5:40 a.m.   First Just Two of Us, OneOther and I,
Now a Third Brother

    It was always two of us, OneOther and I, but now I had a younger brother that I was afraid of. He just scared me and that's all there was to it. He sometimes seemed to be a full-blown monster. He was always after

99

OneOther or me, and OneOther always ended up being chased. I ended up running out of the house because it was one of his worse days. As he tried to catch us, he looked at both of us, but he went after OneOther most of the time.

I got my daughter and headed for the car. It was an old 1940s or 1950s car with a half-front seat for the driver and a rear seat. Tosya was two years old and did not know anything about any of this at all.

What are the levels of understanding or abilities within each of us, and why would it scare us to move forward into that scheduled experience? The experience of living with OneOther as one has never scared me as a physical reality because it is not an everyday experience but as needed. In other words, I have a watcher in OneOther, and it decides when it is necessary to come forward, not me. It seems in the vision that I am worried about a level that will join us very soon; it will add to what I need to get my work done. It's not new, it is just scheduled to join us when needed.

09/24/98   12:08 a.m.   I have a Gift and a Spiritual Direction

I was in or near the back part of a room when a man came in talking, and he seemed to believe that I had a gift or spiritual direction. He also told me that I would probably never get to speak to Minerva or something like that. As I listened to him, I felt it coming over me, vibrations; I was taken up, taken on a trip somewhere.

She held me in a laying position on my back, and I felt the rush of the wind. I could see it as it passed by us, and soon I felt more vibrations than before. They became very intense all over as she carried me in her hands, moving toward a building that I did not recognize. As we reached the building, she continued to talk to me, and the speed slowed enough for us to enter the building. She used her feet in some way to grab my feet and pull me up and over into a laying position, face down, as we continued.

She took me through a glass window and into a room where there were three women. I saw one woman in each of the beds below me. All of them were looking up but seemed ill. The first woman almost looked like she was inviting me to her—it was how she lay there looking up at me—and it made me wonder what kind of place this was. The second woman lay looking up, but she was sicker looking than the first. And the last woman was a person I knew, and she looked very sick. Each one was sicker than the one before. Then the one carrying me asked what I saw, but I wanted to know some things first: Why were they suffering so much? And why were there only females?

I wonder what was done or what decision was made that ended up with them there.

10/06/98   3:30 a.m.   A Small Whirlwind Sprinkles Gold Dust Directly on Me

I was with another woman, and we were talking about a women and the deaths caused by her in the past. It was a woman I knew well. First, I was with that woman during some of the times when she committed the deaths that she was accused of, but I had not told the woman I was with now. We were riding along as I started to think how close I felt to her. But I still could not tell her. I had to act as if I did not care about her at all.

I was now in a house in a large room without furniture with my friend when I felt the spirit of the woman who really caused those deaths. I felt the air stir, the movement of air collecting into a wind, and it became a small circular motion like a whirlwind. It started to form eight to twelve inches in diameter. At first, it was invisible, but as I talked to it, as I told it we wanted no part of it and to leave, it became visible. It was like a whirlwind made of sand or gold dust, and it got as high as the ceiling and circled only me. It looked like a sand storm, and I continued to talk to it, telling it that it was not wanted. I reached out to it, touched it, and moved my hand inside it to move it. It did move, but only a few feet. I could feel it reaching out to me to communicate. It was saying, "Do not be angry or act angry at me."

3:50 a.m.   This Whirlwind Has Been with Me Nine Years

We were still trying to tell the whirlwind to leave, but it just did not get the idea and would not leave me. It all started about nine years ago, and it would not leave now.

10/28/98   5:45 a.m.   I Held a Lion Cub in My Lap

I was sitting in a room with a couple of people when I looked up and saw a lion cub run into the room, coming straight at me. For some reason,

I did not get too scared. It was only a cub, maybe two or three months old, and it jumped up on me like a playful dog. I expected scratches, but there were none. It got up into my lap, and I began rub its head and back for a long time; I just sat there holding it.

11/09/98   6:21 a.m.   The South China Sea Will Freeze

I was in the area of the South China Sea, and the army was trying to find out why I wanted to go back to Vietnam. They questioned me back and forth about why I wanted to go back. I just told them that I had to get back there, that I had seen so much pain in the lives of those people, and that I saw how the South China Sea was going to freeze and that many would die.

I also wondered if the life of Tina Turner was this bad, and I was thinking all this while being on a boat.

The tie-in in the last sentence to Tina Turner is the truth of the first part about the South China Sea. Is the story about Tina worse than was told on screen?

11/13/98   7:13 a.m.   I Witness This Happening in Tijuana, Mexico, to an Eleven-Year-Old Boy

I lived in Tijuana, Mexico, just across the line. I was eleven years old, and I lived with my father who did what he needed to in order to make money. This particular day I was with my father in a bar as he talked to men he knew. I was just sitting there, and in came a man who my father knew, but he sat at another table. I thought that was funny, because he normally sat with my father.

Then some men walked in and just shot him dead. As I daydreamed, sitting there, about what I wanted to eat, my father lay dead on the floor. They grabbed me, and then I was with them. They went to another food shop, and as the shooter walked in, he threw something into the trash can, but what he threw did not go in the trash, so he stepped back to get it and try again. I was just following them. I saw food and cakes of all kinds; my favorite was Hostess CupCakes, and I reached up and got two. I did not have any money, and I just followed them as they walked on, leaving me there. As I came out of the shop one of them was sitting in a little waiting area for customers and the other man was by the door. They showed me a table where I could sit and eat my cake, and I told them I was ready to do whatever I had to do—anything.

I watched this whole thing happen to this young kid, a child who grows up fast to be a young man. He saw his father killed and did not even care that the two men he was with now did it. He only saw it as a way out for him, and he would have done anything to get out.

11/17/98   6:29 a.m.   Tosya Drowns and Has a Metal Rod Sticking in Her Chest

Tosya, my daughter, and I were at the beach, and it seemed so crowded with swimmers and fishermen all together. Tosya was about three or four years old, and she was in so much of a hurry to get in the water—she was in it before I was ready to get in. After a short while, I got her out of the water. Everyone else was going inside except us and one other couple who I knew. Without me knowing it, Tosya had jumped back into the water, and it only seemed like a minute when I heard her cry out, "Daddy!" I ran to the edge of the water, and I saw her go under a second time. I just stepped out on the water without even thinking and walked to her; my feet were only inches under the water. I could see her looking up at me, and her hand reached for me from under the water. I bent over and grabbed her arm, pulled her up fast, and carried her back to shore. My ankles never went under the water.

When I got her back on the beach and lay her on a table, I saw a metal rod sticking through her chest from one side to the other. The drowning part was over, but now the metal rod had to be dealt with, and so I positioned her on the table with my friend helping, knowing I had to do something fast. My friend gave me some alcohol pads to clean around the area, but I had to get it out, so I lifted her up again in my arms and pulled the metal rod out. Now I was scared; I could hear air coming from her chest as she tried to breathe. Her lung had been punctured.

With Tosya in my arms, I did not know what else to do, and as I started to think about the Father///, my friend touched my arm. It was then that something embraced the three of us, and I knew it was the Holy Spirit. As I said, "Thank you," the Holy Spirit/// healed us all at once. In my right ear from behind me, I heard a voice say, "Thank you, too." It was my friend.

11/30/98   6:49 a.m.   The Art of Acupuncture

I was with a group of students training in the art of acupuncture. These students were all young ladies except for the teacher and me. The subjects were young women who lay on tables completely naked. The trainer timed you as you inserted the needles into them and removed them. He then called me, and said, "It is your turn to insert them and retrieve them." Needles were being inserted from the head down to the kneecap area, and I was worried that I might hurt the young lady.

12/12/98   3:32 a.m.   Someone Asked Me What State I Was In, and I said "Blank, Nothingness"

I was riding on the parkway coming home in very heavy traffic, and as I tried to get into the proper lane on my bicycle, everything changed. All of a sudden, I was in a temple of some kind with my friend, and we seemed to be a part of a ceremony of some kind that had two men stationed up front. One of them talked to us, asking us how we felt. Then my friend was asked to sound a bell of some kind, but it was really a cymbal type of sound. When that was done, we had passed two ceremonial stations. We started to the third ceremonial station where we were turned away from the larger ceremony as it continued. Two women then came over and knelt down with me. A little girl who was with them seemed to do all the talking. The women asked my condition. We were still turned away from the leader of the ceremony so we could reflect. The child gave me a mask—a series of masks or faces—and I was to choose which to put on. The women guided me, showing me a square drawing in front of me at eye level. It was black, and the surface was bumpy, and I was told to feel the surface. One of the two women asked me if I was in deep thought or in a trance, and I responded, "I do not know what I am in; it just seems like nothingness, blank."

The little girl walked in front of me the whole time, and then she fell backward and her head hit a knife. I felt her head, and it was fine. I did not know why she fell or how the knife did not hurt her. She continued to talk to me as if nothing had happened, and they continued to ask me where I was and how I felt.

4:21 a.m.   Still in a Room in a State of Contemplation

I was in a room again that was dark except for one candle, and in my mind, I outlined the flame and glow kneeling all the time while I was left alone to contemplate.

8:37 a.m.   Singing and Walking Corner to Corner on a Quilt

I heard a song in my head, and I started to sing it as I walked across the garden I had planted out of old rotten fruit and vegetables that I had found. I planted them in my yard, and it was not long before everything had grown. It covered almost all of the yard. As I sat out in the garden on the ground with Mama, something caught my eye. I saw peppers and other small plants under the leaves of the larger plants just growing there. I touched Mama and showed her the wonderful things I saw, and I was actually surprised to find them.

Then I found myself in the yard alone, and my garden had changed into a quilt. It covered all four corners of the yard and everything in between. I walked around on it, and I started singing, *"For his eye is on the sparrow and I know he watches me, I sing because I am happy, I sing because I am free, for his eye is on the sparrow and I know he watches me."* I just kept singing and walking from one corner to the other corner, making all four corners.

Book XIII

12/16/98   4:30 a.m.   A Three-Inch Power Pack Gives Life

I was in my grandfather's house, there to do a job, and a couple of women walked in. One of them I was to perform some work on. This woman had a power pack that gave her life, so we started to talk about it—about it being removed for me to do the redesign she wanted. She had a female friend with her but would not trust her with the power pack during the operation. She did not know who to trust with her power pack, and so I told her, "Grandma trusted me," and with those words, she said, "I will also trust you," and I pulled the power pack out. She gave up life as she knew it until I put the power source back in, and then she became alive again.

The power pack was about three inches in diameter, and I took it into a small room off the main room to hide it from OneOther who was also there. The house was very old, and I could not find a place that suited me to hide it.

12/20/98   7:31 a.m.   Water Runs from a Tree Stump

We were standing outside looking at a tree that grew up like a stump—no more than ten inches high. I took a hatchet and split it in the middle, and water flowed from it for a long time. I wondered why there was so much water in such a small tree trunk; it looked deformed. The stump was on the edge of a vast open area and very little ever grew there.

It was weeks or maybe months later when I saw all kinds of plants growing in the same area, and I wondered who, or what, let them grow then but had kept them from growing before.

To me, this vision is about discovering the power within to share—discovering that something, or someone, with what looks like very little promise, can end up with so much to give that others can use. The schedules of such things are beyond us to conceive.

12/25/98	3:50 a.m.	I Will Pass On and OneOther will Take My Place

I was at home, and I started to listen to sounds made by me. There were waking up sounds and going to work sounds—the sounds of reaching another level. I had thought earlier about our oil stove and how sometimes we had to switch from one fuel to a different kind. As I listened to my head and the sounds it was making, it was a new level of sound. It was then that I saw in my bed, where I had just gotten up from, one just exactly like me. He was a different level, and he seemed afraid, scared. I began to talk to him, and he touched me as I put my head against his head. The sounds in his were many levels above mine. The sounds began to make my head vibrate, and I knew I had to do something. I began to talk to him about moving to a higher level; he wanted to go.

Then he held me, and I felt a little afraid, but I continued to talk to him. He put his head against mine, as I had done to him, and the sounds collected in his head were unexplainable. I continued talking to him, and that's when another power began to move us both. I was made to lie out just like him on the bed. The power moved me, it made my body circle his as he lay there on the bed. Then I was stopped and positioned at the low end of the circle, and put on the floor with my hands in a position to pray. Just for a moment I did not know if I was supposed to pray, but I did, and then it was over, finished, and he passed on, and I was then here. It was my Father///.

This is about the two that were separate yet together. Now the separation is removed, and the one acts with the present knowledge of both. Praying, yes, and asking for guidance and being thankful for all blessings are the next steps.

01/04/99	3:47 a.m.	Three Levels of Thought and Their Meanings

I was shown different subjects and told that each had three different meanings or levels of thought. I was also shown how to get the facts from each level or meaning as it showed three different ones but similar.

01/05/99   7:30 a.m.   Three Major Levels of Faith and
Understanding

I was shown the actual levels of faith and what we believed or could conceive at each level—our ability to hold fast or simply not understand. I was shown the different levels of understanding that we all get from the same information, but understanding that for each of us, it is different, and I could see those differences.

01/17/99   3:48 a.m.   I Feel Vibrations, and Then I Am Lifted to
the Stars

As I got into bed, that feeling came over me: the vibrations. I was taken, moving fast in a laying position on my stomach, moving up faster and faster. I started to see stars, lots of stars, faster and faster, and then she (the one who was taking me) changed her position from guiding and pulling me up to pushing me from underneath. I was still in a laying position, facing all the stars as I moved through them, and it was so dark and the stars were so bright, and there were so many of them.

It is like Mama, she walked holding my hand, but as I got nearer to my destination, she made me walk out in front of her, and she gave me a push or nudge to go on.

01/20/99   4:09 a.m.   Two Men, One Here and One Gone

This was a very short story about two men, one here and one gone. The question asked by those who knew them and other onlookers was, "What is he really trying to do?" It was the same question the two men in their time asked themselves, and the answer was, "I do not know the answer to the question. I know this has to be done." The answer would be the result, which would not be seen by either man but by others. This night, the second man would go on a trip or journey, as did the first, and the result was unknown to him, but he must make the trip.

In the middle of the night, with a bowl full of pork rind strips, he got into his car and drove off for a trip he had to make. The family looked on and wondered what would he do. Just as before, he was last seen standing in the middle of an intersection, waiting for what would take place next.

This vision tells me to first look at December 25, 1998, in that a man certainly in this story would not have been what was expected in this life before this night. But he was the choice, just as it was before. He seemingly was nothing special in any way, but he was the choice.

01/27/99   3:53 a.m.   My Horse Waits, Nothing Is Holding Him but He Waits

I was outside on a farm, standing on a hillside overlooking a very large field—acres and acres—and I watched my dog run around. I saw a horse off in the distance. It was a lone horse, running toward me very fast, but it was still a good ways off. It kept coming my way and did not slow down at all. When it got within a hundred feet of me, it began to slow down and make a circle around me, closing the circle as it went around me quite a few times. It then fell on its knees, seemingly out of breath, and I knew I could ride him. He had a bridle on him and was ready to go.

Many years ago, I had had a horse that was wild, and as I held its reins in my hand, the horse ran off. Now this one had come to me. I walked him to the house, which was Uncle Herbert's house. I wanted to put him in the barn, because the fenced area where Uncle Herbert had horses was mostly broken down. even though the horses never left it.

I met a cousin who I used to play with. I had not seen him in many years, and we hugged and I asked him about the rest of the family. He was very old now but still doing well, and he came with gifts for me: two large boxes. The two boxes were mine from many years ago, but I had never known about them.

I woke up the next morning, went into the kitchen, and asked Mama if the horse was still out there. I had not put him in the barn or tied him up. She said yes. He was not tied up or anything; he was just standing there waiting on me.

01/31/99   6:04 a.m.   Working with Kids and the Community Center

I was walking down the street as kids were playing on the sidewalk and in the street. They looked to be about five to seven years old. The kids started in on me, following me, pulling on me, and asking many questions until I stopped and talked to them. I told them that they should go to some boys or girls club or community center somewhere and now they wanted me to take them. I decided to take them, but I had to see their mothers first. I took them to the community center where they played stick hockey and other games.

I went in with all those boys and girls behind me. The kids inside were all about thirteen to seventeen years old. I began to explain why we were there. The kids had to talk it over first, right there in the front of us. They decided it was okay, and that they would work with the kids, but when the leader asked who would take an application to the parents and get it signed, no one answered. I said, "I will do it," and they all agreed. I got up and gave a little speech to all of them. I could hear myself talking, and it sounded all right. The last part of the speech went something like this, "I think it's a great opportunity for these kids to be hand in hand with all of you; you will teach them how to be young men and women. Then one day, they might become as close to you as this little lady is to me." The little girl had sat in the row in front of me, on her knees in the chair with the chair turned facing me. Her face was so close—it wasn't three inches from mine. When I said that, everyone laughed, and the little girl got down fast.

02/05/99   7:21 a.m.   Computer Enhancer Module for Electric Cars

We were in Orange County. This time it was Dad and a friend of his. They had driven down and gotten into trouble with a shady auto dealer. They knew what to get and how to get it—a computer enhancer module for an electric model vehicle. The module was four inches by three inches, and they bought it under the wrong conditions. It was against the law to purchase it except through an authorized dealer. They also got away with shortchanging the man too, and if the guy caused them a problem, they were going to turn him in.

That part was like a small hard drive for computers. It made an old system seem like a new one. All cars were electronic, not half and half.

02/26/99   5:13 a.m.   Lifted and Taken to the Stars

I was with others in a van headed home. We had three guys in the van. The van stopped, and one of them wanted to get out and talk to a clerk in a carryout. He came back with a woman who was the clerk he went to talk to, and he said that she wanted to go with us. I said to bring her if she wanted to ride. I started to think about this trip we were on and why I even decided to go on it with them in the first place.

Then I found myself walking on a back country road going west, and I started to think I could not get very far on foot. So when night came, I thought I could get up in a tree to be off the ground for safety. As I kept walking, I saw a house off in the distance and as I got close to the house, I saw a dog in the road and a woman in front of the house.

I felt I just wanted to get above the dog and continue going in the same direction, so I lifted up and started flying off the ground about a hundred feet. That's when I started to see many structures: houses and buildings all made of wood, with odd shapes. I thought I would never forget the way they looked. I looked up in the night sky and saw stars. I said, "I want to go all the way to them," and almost immediately hands grabbed my hands, and we were off to the stars. Just like before, I was positioned in front of her as she held me from behind, and as we started, she told me that we would go all the way through a star this time—that we would go through one, and I would feel something different but be calm. As we got closer, I began to see each star as a sign of the zodiac. As I looked at all of them, I mostly saw crabs for some reason, but they were all brilliant in color.

5:41 a.m.   Baseball in Washington, DC

I heard a "used to be" baseball player say, "I am going to make you a diamond," and I did not think he meant jewelry or a baseball diamond in Washington, DC.

I guess, in hindsight, that he did mean a baseball diamond in Washington, DC.

02/28/99   11:22 a.m.   ROR—Roving Orbital Robot for Deep Probing Missions

I was with an away team on the planet below, and we were getting chemical samples and trying to figure out the best position for our probe. The probe was called the roving orbital robot (ROR), and they wanted him to start working now and to last as long as possible, sending information when scheduled. I said, "Plant him deep in the planet's crust, and when the planet modulates (has a chemical orientation suitable more to our lifestyle), he will surface and begin to give us data. We do not know when, but his body structure is indestructible, and his power system, if not used, will not diminish. He can stay there a thousand years and then surface to triangulate all current planetary objects in the area, sending the most recent readings of his position and the chemical analysis to us.

However, all of a sudden, there was a flash of light, and our ship was gone from the sky. Just for a minute, I thought it had blown up. Then we noticed two lights, two ships. One after the other came into view, and we rushed to finish our work. No matter what, ROR will do its job.

03/04/99   5:42 a.m.   First Light Was Fixed, and Then I Can
Meet All the People of the Earth

First, they tried to fix light, making it so everyone could see it, and it was done. Then the decision was made to let him live until he met all the people of the world, and the answer was, "Yes, he may live until he meets all the people of this world." But one said, "It may take him a hundred years." Then that was fixed, how?

This vision seems to be saying that everyone needs to be able to see the light or what the light represents, and somehow that was made possible. Then something I asked for was to meet people from all over the world, but it seems it will even surpass that. The question of how long all this would take came up, and it is a good thing that it is this day and time in the era of today's technology that this will start.

03/05/99   1:44 a.m.   My Father/// Raises Me Above Them and
Takes Me in a Circle over Them

A group of us were working in the penthouse equipment room when I got a call to come down to a meeting room on one of the floors. As I entered the room, I saw some of my team there. I was looking for a place to sit down as the president, a woman who was a black, started to talk about space and our team working in the penthouse. As she talked, she seemed to become happier for some reason and told us we could go back to work in the penthouse—that she had what she needed.

Before I could make a move, I was grabbed by my upper shoulder area and raised up in the air above the others' heads. I felt this time that it was the Father/// doing this. He/// took me around the room in a circle above the others, and I heard a man say, "There he is, that's the one," as though I was the one that was doing something or causing something to happen.

Then I was taken to a cinderblock wall and taken through it very slowly. It looked like it was magnified one thousand times, as if a cinderblock was ten feet wide. I could see how the cinderblock was made, and I could see every grain in it, everything. The whole time I stayed very still. As we entered a store through its wall, I could see it was a cookie store with very bright lights.

Left and Right Hand Backside

04/11/99   3:39 a.m.   Vibrations within Start like a Jet Engine at Low Idle

I was in the bedroom going over thoughts in my mind when I heard the sound of furniture cracking under pressure. It was loud enough that I stopped thinking about the thoughts within, and I just let my mind wander. I knew that I should do that.

After a while, I felt a low vibration over my whole body, like a jet motor at idling speed. It felt smooth in sound and then it revved up slowly and got to a level that made my feet feel as if they were raised up a little. Then it went to another level and three-fourths of my body was up off the bed. I was being turned out over the floor area with my neck and head still on the bed. I felt the vibrations throughout my whole body, as three-fourths of my body was up because of the level of vibration. It all continued until it reached a body-changing pitch, and when I moved, I felt it through my whole body.

04/21/99   5:13 a.m.   Army Hand-Held Weapons with Ejection Problem

I was in an overseas area at an army base, where I had some responsibility for handheld weapons. It seemed to me that we had small problems with each one of them. The problem was the slide action barrel and the ejection mechanism. There were thousands of these handheld weapons, and I needed to do something. I met with my commanding officer and got orders to return stateside to get some answers. When I got stateside, I went to see a friend who was responsible for parts inspection and for trying out the weapons. He introduced a couple of other people and his commanding officer, but soon they all left, but I did not. I noticed a workbeach when I came in, and I figured I could look firsthand at the weapons. I found the problem and how to fix them right there. They returned to find out what happened to me and caught me at the table.

04/24/99   10:17 a.m.   Television in 3-D

I was looking at television in 3-D. It was like cartoons but more lifelike. The show I was looking at had a host named Brown. He was the black man who hosted the NFC game day program. The other show was regular television—a comedy with Marlon Wayans starring, and he played a person who was pregnant, but this was not in 3-D.

04/26/99   9:34 a.m.   I May Have To Go Back to the Garden of Eden

I was thinking out loud, "I may have to go all the way back, all the way to the beginning, to the Garden of Eden." Then a white lighted area appeared, like a blank television screen, and as it started to clear, I saw a face; I saw my face as a young schoolboy. I had my hands under my chin, and I was looking out the window seeing all the possibilities and wondering when I would take my part, or what part would I play in all this.

Then I saw my face a second time, a bit older, with the same look on my face. Time had gone by, and I was then thinking about retirement. It was 1999 or 2000 and retiring then would not afford me enough money to do what I wanted to do. I saw the United Way building from across the street, and I wondered if a spaceship could land between the two buildings; I thought it could. *This vision was informing me, but at the same time, it was understood I would not pay much attention to it then, in 1999, because my normal retirement date was June 2012. But in 2009-2011 when all these visions came alive to me, I would be able to understand the rest because of this one. You see, my retirement date from United Way Worldwide was December 30, 2010, and using the Mayan calendar of eleven years, that would be about right.*

The spaceship landing between the two buildings means my ship has come in, and the two buildings have a personal meaning to me. I have always referred to the United Way building as being in two sections, the north and south buildings, and the south building was just renovated in 2009 and 2010—between the old and new. The United Way building had to be renovated first in my dream of retiring, but we could only do the south building at the time. It did give me a date for retirement and a full start with this life's work.

04/27/99   1:38 a.m.   The Force between My Hands

I was in the repair shop working with others on vehicles, when I got the idea of taking my hands and circling them, not too far apart from each other, just in a small circle. I continued doing this, and I began to feel a force created between my two hands. I had it and did not know what I had or what to do with it. I began to feel things give and take around me, I continued to move my hands until the very vehicles around me started to move a little. I could see the effect, and I was a little scared.

I stopped and thought about a push-and-pull motion with my hands, and it began to work as I pushed away and then pulled toward me and then went back to the circular motion again. I started to feel a ball shape, and it had force. I would do the push-and-pull motions holding the ball shape. It started to move with force, pushing out things around me and pulling them back in; the cars started to rock side to side. I could see it and feel it until I heard a voice say stop. It was one of the mechanics working under a car, and he cried out, but it was so much force by then that even though I stopped it, it continued for a while. The car moved more violently until there was no sound from under the car.

04/27/99   6:33 a.m.   Left Hand Backside

04/28/99   12:13 a.m.   I See Stars and Other Objects

I was in my bed when I felt something try to turn me over, I felt I must have been lying wrong, so I woke up and actually turned over and went back to sleep. I felt the feelings of mini vibrations, and it was as if everything was fine-tuning itself, and then I was taken away fast, going somewhere.

I was taken at a great rate of speed, faster and faster through the night sky, until I started to see stars and other colorful objects. I felt the speed and force of traveling so fast. I traveled facing backward the whole trip, seeing where we had been instead of where we were going. I felt myself being turned, although I did not think about it, and I saw the stars and other objects come from behind me, passing us as we traveled for a long time just looking at stars.

Then she began to take me back toward the earth, and she sat me down inside a fenced-in chicken coop. Then she faced me again, and this time it was my daughter Tosya. I was standing in the chicken coop, and outside in the yard two women were talking. I knew they saw me, but I did not have anything I could say. I guess Tosya left me something to remember.

I do not seem to have to worry about where I am going, all that will take place for me, and the chicken coop represents the place that I will wait for all this to start. A protected area but a little odd to others. It also seems my daughter is a little over protective when it comes to me.

05/02/99   3:13 a.m.   I Decided to Fly by Myself a Second Time

I was in bed when I decided that I wanted to fly and see the stars by myself. I did not feel a vibration or anything like that, but I went anyway. I did not go through any walls. I just remember rising up into a flying position and gaining a good rate of speed, but I did not see any stars, just a round, gray ball. I saw the ball and then a jet airliner close to me, too close. I was not sure that I was even ready to fly solo yet, and I became a little scared. They were so close to my flying path that I decided to reverse my direction and head down. When I got close to the ground, I started to feel I should try it again. I began to gain speed and rise up, and I woke up. (See "My First Flight," 1976)

05/04/99   1:14 a.m.   Stood on a Rock and Told to Wait

First, I was in very large room with a high ceiling. There was a swimming pool in the room that had pressured water flowing into it from eight to ten different directions. Someone had left me there, and I was supposed to stay until he returned, but in this swimming pool, there were three or four snakes. I keep my eyes on them as I stood on the rock, waiting for the one that left me there to return.

Then I stood with another that I saw yet could not describe. We were on a rock foundation that came up out of the water on one end of the pool. I continued to see the snakes in two places below me, but I was too scared to move from my place. The one with me did move, and it scared me, because the snakes also moved. We threw things in the water and stirred it up good for some reason.

I stood on that rock a long time, and then the one who left returned and got into the water; lying on his side, he trapped all the snakes. He got all the snakes and then left. I finally got down into the water and waded through to the far side, and that's when I recognized where the water was coming in. I remembered the place from many years ago.

05/10/99   3:27 a.m.   I Need Proof I Can Foretell the Future

I was discussing with someone how I could foretell the future, and she suggested I write down everything because it would be hard to prove otherwise. Therefore, I will write everything down with dates so in thirty days, when it is revealed, I will have it documented to show others.

This vision is telling me something that has already been happening, but it also is putting me on notice that everyone else will also see the eleven-year and nineteen-year calendars when they take place. This book is part of the eleven-year and nineteen-year calendars, said to be the twenty-year calendar the Mayans used. It works to see what took place in 1992 and after will also take shape again in the area of 2011 and 2012.

5:36 a.m.   I Am at a Children Center in Africa

I was at a children's center in Africa. I was inside with the children, and one of the little boys was in trouble; the police or security people had come for him. They wanted him for some reason. I talked to them for a long time, telling them the boy was only playing with the kids here at the center. They took the boy anyway, and my associate told me they had to, but we then found out that they were not police at all, and I wondered why they wanted him.

I rushed out to stop them. Two tall men showed their guns and started inside the building. I stopped them; I said, "No guns." That's when one of them pointed a gun at me not five feet away. It felt strange to see a barrel pointed in your direction when you know what a gun can do. That's when I started to talk to them fast. One of them said he would fight with me, and he put his fists up to fight, but I said, "What can I do to you? Nothing." He then said, "My women will go in and take care of the matter; they will do whatever it takes." I said, "Don't you care about the children? They could get hurt." He got very mad and tried to grab me, but his partner was between us and kept us apart as I just continued to talk. Then the tallest one said, "He's got a funny voice," pointing at me as I just kept talking.

05/17/99   5:09 a.m.   Light Travel Platform from Point to Point

We had a small problem: a goose that weighed one hundred and fifty pounds and was about four feet tall. It got here okay—and now we needed to beam it out of here. The Washington and Montgomery Street light travel platform—that was where we would beam the bird out to another place around the world. We could beam point-to-point on earth, or point-to-space station and return. The person who did all the work to get the bird inside the platform enclosure did it with candy, and the bird loved it. We had to be sure everything was ready, because it would take us a while before we could try it again if we messed this one up. We were ready and finally beamed the bird away, and it worked just as it should have.

The Washington Street area was jammed with cars—nothing moving at all. The man who led this project was Spanish American, and when I last saw him, it was in the newspapers, and he looked great. Today, I went to his home to see him. He was sick in bed, and he had been sick for a while. His face, normally white, had turned dark, and the lines on his face had all gotten deeper; he looked so worried about something. I wish I knew how to help him or knew what caused his problem.

05/25/99   5:23 a.m.   Right Hand Backside

05/30/99   7:56 a.m.   An Egyptian King's Throne Made like an
                         Airship

I went out to Merrifield in Fairfax, Virginia, where a friend of mine owned an equipment warehouse where I used to buy hydraulic equipment. When I got there, it seemed the name had been changed to T. H. something. I walked around, and I thought it was closed, but then I saw a door that looked like it might be open. It was open. It took me back to my childhood—the place looked like a toy store to me with all of the equipment.

When I was a kid, I dreamed about flying cars. I told Mama about it, and she sat down to hear my dream. I was remembering that as I walked around inside. I saw a showroom the size of a football field full of hydraulic equipment, but nobody was around.

I have always heard a voice. I like listening to it talk to others, but this day it would be different. I thought about a warehouse like this for myself. I walked back to the parking lot, and I heard that voice again. As I stood there in the parking lot, I saw something in the sky that I could not make out at first. I saw some kind of spaceship come down and land in the field. I ran to hide behind some trees, and I continued watch it. The ship was shaped like an Egyptian Pharaoh's throne with a man king sitting in it, and it opened up and men dressed in a uniform of some kind got out. I covered myself so they would not find me, but in a short time I felt footsteps close to me and then a hand on me, which stood me up quickly. I saw they had something for me to wear. It was a purple and white robe. The man who dressed me was bald headed, and like a warrior type who stood by him in full dress armor, he was all armor too. I heard the voice within me talking again, this time talking to me, and I said aloud, "They have come for me." I was willing to go with them.

06/05/99　2:38 a.m.　Father///, I Commit My Soul to You///

I was in my vehicle headed toward Duke Street, on Route 236 going west, when I saw a friend, and she was talking to someone in a car at the traffic light. I stopped at the light, and then all the cars pulled off, and I heard her say something about me giving her a ride, so I stopped again to pick her up, but as I put my foot on the brake, there were no brakes at all, and the pedal went straight to the floor.

Now the road was not the street I expected to be there, and it got worse, because now it was not even a road anymore. I went through a dense wide green bush, a single bush that I could not avoid for some reason as it was spread across my path. I still had no brakes. I began to see houses being built. There were many large estates with plenty of space around them. Then I saw a second green bush that was the same as the first, and I could see it was the end of the path.

I saw the cliff in front of me, and the ocean far below, I pushed the brakes, even though I had none earlier when I had tried to stop. I just decided to pray. I prayed saying, "Father///, I commit my soul to thee///, and I believe in you///." I went off the edge of the cliff, and it was a long way down to the bottom.

I saw swimmers looking in my direction, and they began to run toward where my car would have come down, as I now only saw things from the swimmers' perspectives and not my own. They ran to the car, but they slowed as the car came into view. It was bent up beyond repair and smoking, and they attempted to turn it over on its rims, but it did not work.

4:07 a.m.　I See the Life of a Family and the Father's Problems

I was looking at a family from just above them, and I saw the father was having many problems. I also saw he had three kids, a girl and two boys. I saw he was very mad and frustrated about something. This man was built like a football player, and I saw what he could do when he was angry.

I saw him get mad and throw his son, who was only five years old, down on the floor. I saw him do this a couple of times. I started to talk to him, and he did listen for a while, but then he would do the same thing all over again. His daughter, who was six, ran and grabbed him because he was standing over the small boy on the floor beating him as if he were a grown man. He did not stop when she grabbed him, but the older boy, who looked to be about ten years old, grabbed him too. The father then realized that the kids were all trying to stop him, and it was then that he stopped. He heard me. I said, *"They are right to stop you from hurting your son; you now see you need help yourself."* We continued to talk, and he agreed that together we would start to look for his help.

I talked and walked as he followed me, and we took the same road as in the 2:38 a.m. vision. As we walked, the road turned into the path again, and I continued to talk to him about the help we were looking for him. I did not know where on this path we would find it, but I did know it was on this path, and it would happen for him. As we walked, I saw the houses all built up now, and a new library with beautiful lawn around it. He began to walk in front of me on the path. I also saw a beautiful brown and tan puppy on his left, but he got interested in the library. I was trying to lead him down the path, but he walked toward the library. I now saw two puppies, both the same color and size. One sat still for me to pet him, and the other was in front of the young father as he headed to the library. I wanted to continue down the path with him, but he went into the library. I hoped he would find help there.

06/09/99   6:34 a.m.   Four US Presidents Meet to Talk at a House in the Woods

I was with a small team, and I had no idea why we were out in the country. We were in a four-wheel-drive vehicle, driving off the main road to a side road. We went down a very steep hill that seemed to go straight down. I have never seen a road go straight down like a carnival ride. We were looking for something, but I did not have a clue as to what it was.

We stopped, and I was looking at a small house in the woods. Inside it, we could see four presidents sitting at the table, including the present one of the day. Then, I was standing to one side of the present-day president as they talked.

Later we were back in the four-wheel-drive vehicle, leaving that place and going out the same road. I saw both sides of the road coming from the top of the hill down into this valley. We were in a four-wheel-drive vehicle that had the monster-sized wheels that could drive anywhere. As I saw the hill that looks like a mountain, I started to think that we could never make it back up that hill with all of the tall, green saw grass on both sides of us.

Then we were on the main road, and we saw a state police car up ahead of us. It had pulled someone over, and we slowly passed it and entered a small town. Immediately we saw police at a school crossing. It was so close that it was hard to stop in time. The next thing I knew I was standing in line in a DMV. I had a sidearm under my coat; I had clearance but they did not know it, and I was thinking about how to notify them about it, but they did not seem to care.

06/10/99   3:37 a.m.   My Fight with a Dragon

I was fishing with others in a place I did not really know. We all had lines in the water, and some of us had two lines in. I finally got a bite on both my lines, and I pulled both of them at the same time. I stood there with two rods, both bent badly, and not able to reel in either one. I needed help from somebody, anybody. I saw a white women, and I called her. She came over but she had a baby she was carrying. I looked around and I saw a black woman, and so I called her. She came forward, and I gave her one of the rods, but it did not have a reel on it, and it was beginning to break.

I started to reel in what I had on the line. I tangled other lines out there, but I just kept reeling it as fast as I could until I began to see two large fish instead of one. I continued to reel it in until it got close enough to almost touch. I then saw it was not a fish at all, but a dragon, and it was a big one. I had hooked a dragon with an enormous head on the end closest to me, but it also had a serpent-type head on the tail end. I grabbed the dragon with both hands and started pulling on it to get it on shore. Then I saw another dragon behind it. I had two dragons on one line.

I continued to pull on it, and I had it almost on shore. It must have been the mother, because the one behind it was a little smaller. I saw that

I did not really have it hooked on anything; it had just followed the other one in. I just about had the mother on shore, but two was a problem, because the baby was almost as big as the mother. The whole time, the gray-looking serpent's end or tail was trying to strike me. I actually wanted to let it go, but I was so tangled up that I could not. If I lost my grip on it, it could get me.

The baby dragon just hung around in the water near the shore. I thought I had two of them until they surfaced. I did not have the one totally out of the water yet, and I guessed the baby would just go back into deep water once I got the mother on shore.

06/15/99   I See a Brilliant White Light and Then Nothing

I was out with others in a car near Gum Springs. I heard from those in another car that they had had a run-in with the law and were almost caught. I did not know what they did, but I found out they were after a woman in the car. Two were in the car now, Tosya and another woman. The police wanted that woman bad, and I was wondering what woman it could be.

It was then that it first happened. Off in the distance was a brilliant white light without any sound. Then, for a short time there was nothing—all the sounds around us stopped. I guess others were looking at it, just as we were. Then you could see it, it was like a great wave, two hundred feet high or higher, and it was coming—knocking down everything that it passed, and stopping just short of us.

We could see the white light coming from the east northeast, and everyone stopped their cars, got out, and ran for cover. Cars, houses, everything was blown away or destroyed, and during all this I thought about that one police officer who wanted the woman; he really wanted her bad.

I had a dog with me. It was just a puppy. Tosya and I kept him with us all the time, but he got loose at the last place we got out of the car near Alexandria. The blast wave had come toward us twice and then we saw it for the third time: the brilliant white light and then the shock wave. It rose up in the sky, coming toward us, and this time passed over us. Three blasts and the white light, then the shock wave, and during this whole thing, we all ran in different directions for shelter. My puppy was running, and I could not find the leash to get him. I noticed he had gotten smaller during the three blasts.

06/20/99   I Stole a Gate Pin I Called It a Key

I was walking with a female friend as we passed a very tall black gate, and I noticed an insert, a pin in the gate, and I wanted it. It was dusk, nearly dark, and I climbed the fence and tried to lift the pin out. It moved and then lifted out easily. I replaced it with one I had that was smaller. I heard something from the house. It sat back off the street a ways, so I just stayed quiet until the noise stopped. I took the larger gate pin and replaced it with a smaller one. No one would know the difference.

We left, but I started to worry about the key being too small and the gate coming off its hinge, so we started to run and then split up. I started to hide the pin and come back later for it. I even thought about mailing it back to them.

Gate Key

10:13 a.m. Left Hand Backside

07/12/99   3:53 a.m.   In New York for Installation of Police Officers

I was in New York for an installation of officer ceremony; I had just been made a New York City police officer assigned to the Golden State Parkway area.

I was at home with my family at North West Street in Alexandria, explaining to them how I got the job. I was a Vietnam veteran, and the New York City Police Department cut a lot of red tape for me and others who wanted to become police officers. I needed to find out my date to report for my first scheduled duty. After the ceremony, we had the day off.

I would call in and have someone look at the duty roster. I felt I had to call in quick because I thought I worked on Monday.

I wanted to get a job in Alexandria, but New York was easier, and I went for it. (See January 25, 1998.)

Police officers had to be hired very quickly because of the officers that were lost.

07/14/99   12:46 a.m.   Move Air between My Hands

I lay in bed half-awake and half-asleep. As I had done months ago, I thought and started moving air with my hands. I started to move my hands, and quickly I felt the force between them. I continued to build it up and then opened my arms, pushing and pulling it in and then out, holding onto it. I started to see things in front of me move a little, and then all of the things began to move as a great force of wind moved across the land. I continued and felt it build until the whole earth top was moving back and forth with the movement of my arms.

I was then taken, as always, on a flight for a while, and then I was returned to my bed. But this time I was returned for only a moment. I was taken up again, and I felt the rush of wind on my body. I saw night turn into day and pass again into night. I saw planes on the ground and then saw one high in the air. I was taken to that plane, which was in flight. I could see it was a military plane. I got close to its wings, and then I was a foot or two from its motor and could read the small writing on it. I could also touch it. I stayed in flight with the aircraft for a long time, and then I was returned to bed.

Then in only a minute it seemed I was taken up in the air again, with nothing around me at all. I was just held there, and I felt my face move under the skin. I felt markings being made on my face as I was being held there. I felt this time that it was the Father/// doing this.

As clear as day, I see my face and the lines being drawn on my forehead. The black blood ran down, and the artist drew as he pleased. I saw myself face-to-face and saw the artist lines as they were drawn on my face. The lines were my days, and then days were my time, and the time was my life in the world.

As I was taken up, I also saw for the first time a vehicle with what looked like a person in it who had been taken at gunpoint. Then I saw emergency vehicles and heard them. (See April 27, 1999.)

1:40 a.m.   A Daniel-Type Vision (Daniel of the Bible)

The voice said only this: "Where you plant your green crops, it will turn to sand and be dry." Then I saw green foods of all kinds, cooked, and sand was being poured over it all. (Very important.)

This tells me that where you have harvested your crops for many years will have to be changed, and if continued, you will be caught without an answer.

07/17/99   6:44 a.m.   Health Insurance Cost

I was outside in a field with my blanket, standing by some water, and it was the backwater of the river going into the bay. It looked like both fresh and saltwater creatures lived in it. I could see an eel and other crawling things. I decided to lie down on the blanket, but I quickly saw little creatures in the water that could crawl out up on the bank.

I moved back as Tosya came, and for some reason we started to talk about insurance: the different carriers and their charges. Tosya told me that one major insurance company charged seventy-five dollars per month and paid everything medically. We talked about the cost of insurance being too high. I guessed that what I had must have been the high one.

7:36 a.m. Health Insurance—How Do We Insure Health Care

How do we insure health or health care? I saw a container, pint-size, colored black and white with green letters, being held in someone's hand. A life insurance company said they were for health care or in some way backed health care for their own reasons.

07/18/99   12:38 a.m.   People Circle Me with Their Hands on My Head

I was in a mall or shopping area, walking with friends. One knew the place and area, but I had no clue where we were. We were walking, and two guys who looked like brothers skated into us. We got past that, and then another guy skated into us, but this guy told us we were supposed to follow him. I wanted to get myself something to eat. Neither one of us knew who he was or why he wanted us to follow him anyway. We were scared not to, and he led us down a back alley. I saw only one white door and then it got dark, but I felt I had better not complain.

We followed him inside a door, and I heard a lot of people. I started to think right away that it could be a gang that might beat us up. When we got into the room, I felt lots of hands on me, and all of the people seemed to be talking or hollering at me. They made a circle around me and all joined hands. Then I felt all of their hands on my head at once, and they said something, circling and talking with all of their hands on my head.

I kept my eyes closed most of the time and said a few words to my Father///, and that was it. I kept quiet and said nothing to anyone. During the time they circled me, I saw a little of the place inside. I saw a man and woman who looked like shopkeepers. They were just looking at what was going on. It was a clear day, but I kept my eyes closed most of the time. Next, I found myself standing by a place that had food, and I asked, "Are you going to feed me?"

7:21 a.m.   The Two with Me Walk on Water

I was with two other people. I had been with my family at the museum in Washington DC earlier, but I had left there with these two people I met, a man and his wife. I was not really sure I knew them. As we walked around, he got a message. He told his wife he had to go to the other side of the park across the water and get something, and I could not hear them very well. Then I heard him say that he had to get something and take it to a friend who needed it right away. They walked right out in the water. As I got in a rowboat and started to paddle, I was watching them walk on water. The two of them were talking to each other and walking as if on land, and I was in the rowboat, paddling as fast as I could to keep up with them. They were up ahead of me, and I hollered out to them, "I didn't know you all were supposed to walk on water." They turned to me, looked, but kept walking. Then they began to go down in the water until it was neck high, and they began to swim. I guess I had said the wrong thing. I really want to tell them that, but when I got to the other side, I just walked over to the Massachusetts Avenue and C Street area where my family was.

07/21/99   6:19 a.m.   A Time in Earth's History When Land Was Divided into Zones

This was a time in Earth's life when all towns and cities were cut up into zones, and if you lived in one zone, you would not be able to travel in another without threat to your life. I met a couple of guys in my zone from the northern zone, and they were in deep trouble. I saw them, and I knew one of them, so I decided to help. This could end up being the biggest mistake I ever made, but I took them to see the people. No matter how much some people like you there are always a few who do not. Some there would do anything to get back at you. Helping those guys, even though the people decided to let them go back to their zone, meant trouble for me.

One day, I wanted to go and see my girlfriend who had visited me weeks before. I wanted to make the trip within the next few days. In our zone, a leader of a small group did not like me at all. I had interfered in something he considered his meat on his turf. He had hunted and bagged some guys from the northern zone a while back and bought them before the people. I was there, and I was against him hurting them. On my way out of the zone, I ran into that guy with his men, and he let me know how he felt about me and that he knew what I was about to do. He told me he hoped somebody in the other zone would roast me. I just looked at him, said very little, and walked on.

As I walked, I first had to pass through property that did not belong to anyone—a place we called "no man's land." When I got into the northern zone, I went straight to the house where my girlfriend was, but she seemed a little standoffish, and I wondered why. Then I saw another girlfriend of mine in the same house; she called to me and pointed to the bedroom. This was not looking too good for me, but someone outside called her. It was another woman, and they were supposed to be going to work somewhere. She would not have time.

I left. I figured I had better get out of there as quickly as possible, but I ran into some northern-zone troops. They grabbed me, and they were just about to see how many parts they could cut out of me, when up walked a guy who was a good friend of mine. He was family to one of the guys who I had helped not too long ago back in my zone. He talked a lot but stopped the whole thing right there. He got me a free pass from them out of the zone. I knew that everyone knew I was there and that I was trying to leave the area. I felt that at any turn I could be met by someone wanting to do me harm. A free pass would not help me if they really wanted to hurt me. He did not say much when he handed me the pass except that he was "returning the favor, and don't come back." He also said, "Don't take too long getting out of the zone either."

Just about a mile from the border, another gang stopped me, and I saw some faces I knew, faces from my past, and they did not like me either. The leader was Drew; like some of the others, he wanted me bad, and the free pass didn't mean much if the troops were not around. I finally found out why I was having so much trouble. Someone in my zone told them I was coming and what route I might take. As I stood there, Drew did not act as if he knew me at all. Then he said, "I have you now," and for the first time I felt really scared.

Then a guy walked up who was one of the guys I had gotten out of trouble, he grabbed my hand and walked me to one side away from them, and he began to talk and cry. He hugged my neck, said he was sorry, and said that he was glad he had the chance to thank me. He got me out of that problem. They pointed the way to my zone, and one of them said, "Yes, it's that way someplace." Then Drew said, "You got away, but you've got some friends waiting for you when you get back."

I knew just who he was talking about; they wanted me worse than any of these guys did, and I was headed right back toward them.

Book XIV

07/24/99   6:18 a.m.   Asian Medicine for Back Pain

(b) I was with others, waiting on a boat of some kind that was crossing the water, when everyone started to call on my friend to hurry. He was still in the canteen, and the boat was about to leave. I turned and ran back to find him still in the canteen's bar area, getting a drink. I took him by the arm, and we ran back to the boat. It started to move a little, and we jumped on. As we walked toward the front of the boat, I had to step up three steps, and as I started up those steps, I saw an Asian man and woman sitting there. I started to pass on the right side of the woman, but I saw it was best to go between them. As I took a step, I gave in to pain in my back that had been there a longtime. As I took my next step, the Asian man reached his hand out and gave me a handful of seeds and parts of plants of all kinds. One handful from him was two handfuls for me.

I bowed in thanks, and I realized I was dropping some of them as I walked on. When I reached Andrea, I asked for some water to take the herbs with.

08/01/99   2:26 a.m.   A Little Girl Knows She Is Dying

I had a little girl just about two years old, and she was dying. Her mother carried her to her casket and lay her in it. She was not yet dead, but so close. I did not want to go close to the casket but was standing a little distance off. I began to say to her in a very low voice, "It is going to be alright." My daughter looked at me as if she heard it. She was not meant to hear it, but she began to smile and get up, I looked at her mother and then back at her. How could I tell her I did not mean she would get well? Now I had to go and hold her until she died. She would not get better, and I did not mean for her to hear me say that.

If my Father///, our Father///, told me in a soft low voice I would be alright, I would believe and get up too. It seems to me the father of the little girl could learn something from her and accept the gift.

08/03/99   6:04 a.m.   Peace in the Valley—It Started There and Must End There

We all sat around together singing "There will be peace in the valley" and just having fun. My friend, Peggy and about seven others sang a lot, but I had to be careful about trying to hit those high notes. There was a lot more going on, but it all started with the valley, and it would end in the valley.

It is not about a song, but it is about history and how it was written. It all started there thousands of years ago, and still we face it today. The question, "If you could stop it all right now, would you? What if on Monday morning, May 19, 2014, we stopped all the wars, the killing in large groups? If we could start to put a peace plan together, all over the world, would you stop if you could? We cannot twist the spirit to make it fit the physical body; it would be a lie.

08/04/99   11:51 a.m.   My Head Sounds like a Broken Washing Machine

I was lying in bed when I began to phase in and out of sleep, and I started to feel many things. The sounds started first, a single sound of a click of a switch coming on. Seconds later, a click, but like Morse code (a short one), and the small motor started up inside my head. It started to run, but all the gears were jamming. Something was wrong, because it sounded like a loud, broken washing machine that my mother used in my childhood days.

Then I started to talk to myself, because for a little bit, even I wanted to stop it. But I knew I wanted to experience it all the way. I went on talking to it, and as I did, my heart sped up. I asked it to slow down for me and it did. The noise in my head also was slowing down, getting better, but it was still a little noisy, as if the gears were rubbing the wrong way. After a while, it stopped, but it never got smooth, and as I lay there with my eyes closed, I was aware of someone walking around me. As the person walked, the person traced the area of my eye sockets and eyes with his or her fingers, first one side and then the other. This was done twice, and the feeling was heavenly. Additional things were done to my face and then only silence; I heard nothing else.

Then somehow, somewhere, I was captured by a group of men, five of them, who tied me up and began talking to me and doing whatever they wanted. After a while, I started to talk back to them saying, "Die, die, die." I just kept saying it until I saw them start to crumble to the floor, all of them together. I got loose and started to leave, but they seemed to get better and get up as I was leaving. The big guy who stood behind me got up and got a shotgun, and he came after me as I headed out of the door.

Outside, I was pinned in by a wire fence all around the place for animals. They saw the police cars with police officers getting out, lots of them. I called to the police officers to help, and a gun battle started, and I ran with one of them still after me.

08/15/99   12:59 p.m.   My Father/// Gives Me a Job to Do
[Not a Vision]

I had just gotten back from church, and I parked in the front of my house, listening to a song called "There Will Be Peace in the Valley Someday." My Father /// said to me, "Your job is to rob, steal, and take back everything the devil/Satan has claimed." I guess that meant I could use any means necessary within my authority.

08/21/99   8:36 a.m.   During the Days of Slavery in the 1700s

I was on a farm. I was not sure where, but I had been here before. As I walked up toward the place, I was met by another black man. The clothing that was worn there told me at least what time period it was. I followed him into the house, and it was filled with black men of all ages. Outside, I saw white men in their late twenties or early thirties, walking in groups of two or three together. The place we were in was part of a large land area with a very large house and many smaller ones all over the place.

We seemed to be in the kitchen where food was being cooked and processed, and a young black man was sitting in a chair by the door as a letter carrier came in. He gave the man sitting by the door the mail, and one of the men gave him two eggs. One of the eggs fell and cracked, but it was hard-boiled. The letter carrier picked the egg up and started to eat it as he left.

Then I saw a half-black man who I knew, and as I started toward him, one of the others pulled me back. Then I saw why—he was also half in charge of the rest of us. He walked right by me, as if he had never seen me before, saying nothing. We had just come in from the fields together.

When it was all clear, the men gave me a jug of strong drink. It was good to me, but I went outside with it, and before I knew it, one of the men with me said, "Gag," and I did. I acted as if I had choked on the stuff or as if it was too much for me to handle. Just then, one of the white men walked up behind me and laughed, but no one else did.

This place and time had to be in the 1700s; we did not approach or speak to a white man, and we never saw any black or white women.

08/26/99   5:02 a.m.   Police Give Up on Drug-infested Area

I was a commander with the police force, and I was taking five units on patrol in a part of town that was drug infested. We drove three cars, one car to a street going in a westward direction, and behind us three blocks were three more cars. All of us were driving Prowlers, which was what the police cars were called. When we hit the drug area, we got out and went on foot for the next half block. Kids were everywhere, ages six and seven all the way up. They were all here, nothing but kids—and more white kids than any other. You could shine the flashlight in a dark space and see them running, trying to keep the light off them.

We had spread out, and we got to a big old house with no lights. There were square holes, tunnel-like, that were dug in the side of a hill by the house, and people were trying to live in those mounds. I looked around and all my officers were gone. A little girl came out of the house saying, "You've got to help her; they have her upstairs." I could see my team going back to their cars, doing nothing. I saw another officer standing on the hill, looking like a black Hitler in a police uniform. I told him to let the team stay here, but he wanted them out. There were all these problems here, and we were going to just leave it all alone.

08/27/99   8:53 a.m.   The First Time I Visited Earth

I was in a spacecraft. The navigator was dead and had been dead for a long time. The ship was just large enough for two. It landed on this planet at a time when the big animals were just dying out. I simply rode in the craft and did nothing else. The ship was programmed to find safe areas to let me out. When I first touched down on Earth it was near the mouth of a cave. We were pulled into it, but the ship did not open and it was able to get away. They were too primitive, and it was not safe; so after a while, the ship moved on.

The ship moved on until we landed near a group that I became scared of because of their size. They were six to seven hundred pounds and tall. They used others of their kind to find explosive devices that look like an Aztec style design or some style like that. The devices were three or four inches across and lay with all the other rocks, but these pieces had shape and purpose. This was the first stop, and I stayed for a while.

I went back to the spacecraft. It lifted off, and it found another place far away from this one, where tomatoes grew wild and died and then grew again.

I remember seeing three places where we stopped. At the third place I stopped, I got out and was taken by the people there. A woman rode a horse, and she looked good; I touched her hair. They picked me up from my craft and carried me on a wooden wheeled vehicle of some kind. I reached out from where I sat and touched and felt the hair of this black woman. I came without weapons. The ship had surveyed the planet until it found this last place.

The places I stopped all had people of some kind, but the first place was too primitive to communicate. The second place was more civilized, and I spent time with them.

Aztec Style Design

08/29/99   5:24 a.m.   It Drilled a Circle in the Center of My Forehead (Third Eye)

I was in my office at United Way. Down the hall, I heard other staff members talking, so I went to the door of my office. I could hear Lee talking in another office. I wanted to know whose office that was; I thought it was Robin's office. I turned around to get a good look at my office, and it was full of stuff.

Before I could sit down, I began to hear buzzing sounds like a bee. It was all around my head as I tried to sit down. I know it was me being worked on, and I was not even lying down. I did not have time to lie down, as the buzzing got so intense. I just sat there. It stopped in the center of my forehead, as if it was shaping or making something, and I knew it was shaping my facial features in some way like before. This felt like a doctor's drill as it seemed to be making a hole in the center of my forehead. Everything was done in the center of my forehead, face, and left side, and I kept still the whole time.

This vision tells me I will be given what seems like a third eye from the Father///.

08/31/99   8:08 a.m.   I See the Evil One Face-to-Face

I was on the third floor with Jim, a friend, and he kept feeling the elevator and walls. He thought he felt heat. I did not. We entered the elevator and went down to the second floor where he got out. I was going to get out, but I started to feel around in the elevator too. When I got out, I walked down the hallway and saw the problem. It was that old troublemaker himself, the one I call Satan. The next thing I knew, I was outside looking around, and I saw three new trash containers placed around the building. I walked to the other side of the building, and I saw three more.

Then I was outside, standing with a Catholic priest and another person that I did not know, and we were all looking up at the second and third floors. We were watching the evil one walk the hallways, back and forth. I started back inside to face him, and I called to the priest, "We need you to pray. Don't be scared, come on."

This part of the building was all new, a complete new addition.

09/03/99   1:28 a.m.   Pharaoh's Seat

I was told just these words: "Pharaoh's seat was a spaceship."

4:08 p.m.   Ezekiel 33 Was Given to Me by Grace/// [Not a Vision]

I was given this bible location to read, "Ezekiel 33," by my Father///.

09/04/99   10:48 a.m.   Pictures of Egypt, Israelites Cities, and a Temple

Running before my eyes I saw framed pictures of Egypt and all that was built. Everything was as if it were in dark shadow or outline. There were many pictures and then blank pictures.

I then saw Israelite cities and the temple, and all was wasted. I saw dead people lying before the destruction—some were soldiers slain in battle. These two groups of pictures connected directly, and there were no people in Egypt at all.

09/05/99   8:53 a.m.   Left Hand Backside

09/17/99   6:35 a.m.   Left Hand Backside

09/18/99   3:08 a.m.   Exodus 14:12:1 Was Given to Me

When Exodus 14:12:1 and one other verse and chapter were given me, it only showed me an insignia or group breastplate. I was being tried by a very strong force that came to me, covered me, and held me as I prayed and called on the name of the of the Father///. I also called the name of Jesus, and it let me go then. This all happened twice.

4:46   a.m.   Left Hand Backside

9:47   a.m.   Left Hand Backside

09/20/99   8:34 a.m.   A Vietnamese Army Soldier Shows Me
                           How the Vietcong Used to Hide

I was walking with my friend in Vietnam. He was a Vietnamese army soldier, and we were talking about the war. Sammy was my friend and he told me how things were done. We walked in a lush green field, full of grass about twelve to fifteen inches tall. It might have been a rice field. Sammy, without talking very much, lay down in the grass until I saw only his head, and then his head was out of sight. He was telling me how the Vietcong concealed themselves from us during the war, and how the soldier walked the fields and never knew they were there until it was too late. Behind him, I saw in the distance a large silvery fish flying and I saw the large body of water it must have come from. Sammy showed me how to conceal myself, first part of the way, and then all the way.

09/25/99   7:17 a.m.   I Sit In a Corner with My Hands over My Ears

I was sitting with my back to the wall, my hands over my ears, trying not to hear anything. I did not want to hear anything.

7:32 a.m.   I See Myself Sitting in the Corner with My Hands over My Ears

I saw myself setting with my hands over my ears, but there was a row of books behind my head, and I thought they were attached to my head in some way.

Book XV

10/03/99   6:29 a.m.   Left Hand Backside

8:11 a.m.   A News Report concerning a Mechanical Robot
[Not a Vision]

I listened to a report on the news concerning the United States losing a mechanical robot in orbit around a planet that it was getting information from. (See February 28, 1999.)

10/04/99   4:50 a.m.   Not Just Law but Justice Too

I was sitting in the living room of a woman and her children as she heard a court case concerning two people. They went through the process and were misled by their lawyers. It seemed that the man and woman took the case to a lawyer, and the firm took the case. During the proceedings, they turned the property and goods of their clients into their holdings. It seemed that the young couple did not know anything about law and the instructions from their lawyers were to turn everything over to them.

The young son of the couple kept on his parents until they went to see another lawyer or officer of the court. This lady was hearing exactly what happened, from her home, as the couple explained it to her. She looked back at me and said, "What do you think?" I told her, "These people have a case, and it should be prosecuted; charge the lawyers." The lady got up from the table where the three of them sat, came over to me, and told me softly that all that had been done. The reason for this hearing was that the lady who was part of the complaint had beat her old lawyer up—that was the reason they met today. Then she kissed me on the lips, and grit or something she was eating got into my mouth. I felt it and let it stay. Today was not just about laws but justice too.

10/15/99   1:08 a.m.   Left Hand Backside

10/16/99   3:52 a.m.   I Started Praying in English and it
                           Continued in Latin

I was walking along when I saw a white female unclothed at the top and not developed much at all. I looked at her, trying to figure out her problem. She was a beautiful young girl with short blond hair. It was explained to me that she had a sickness, and she would not get well. The young girl started to toss and turn. She was saying something in low voice as the one with me continued to tell me about her problem, and I saw it for myself. I heard people off in the distance, and I began to pray for her. As I continued to pray, about halfway through I forgot the words. Without missing a beat, the words continued out of my mouth, but they were foreign words, like Latin, and they continued until the prayer was finished.

Then before I could do anything, I was taken up fast. I still had pennies in my right hand from somewhere. I had something in my left hand too, but felt I must not carry the pennies with me on this trip, so I dropped them down by the young woman. I was taken faster than ever before. I only saw the inside of the inside world and planet systems, which were very close together—so many of them and so vast—like our solar system with a million other systems, grouped one after the other as we passed. That was, until I woke up.

10/21/99   6:13 a.m.   Learning How to Take the Right Action
                         and Apply It in Different Ways

As we talked, I started to get the feeling about how to take a right action and apply it in different ways to fit those in need. Not everything that was right in the sight of one fit all cases, but it made it no less a right, a real obligation, and our obligation was to use all sources for the betterment of people or conditions. This was all done while keeping in line with the path but may not be the normal sighted or experienced way.

11/16/99   12:16 a.m.   OneOther, Myself, and Now There Is Another

I was at home, and we had a guest, a Mr. Smith. I did not like him at all, but he was my girlfriend's guest, so I put up with him. As I watched them sitting on the couch, the two of them were getting too close for me—right under my nose—and I had just about had enough.

I started into the kitchen to get something when I heard something hit the floor behind me. One of them had thrown a fork on the floor right behind me. As I asked my girlfriend about it, he laughed. That made me mad, and I could hear them talking about me as I went into the living room to sit down, but I was so mad I could not sit down—that within me would not let me sit down. I started to feel something I had never felt before, a presence that felt uncontrollable, and it took over my body. I lifted up off the floor two or three feet right, beside the hallway entrance, and I heard him coming out of the room toward me. When he got close, I grabbed him, and he immediately saw me as I threw him from one side of the room to the other. Then I threw him down right at the feet of my girlfriend, and I told him in a voice I had never heard before to leave and never come back.

He left quickly, and minutes later I was okay, but a knock at the door started it again, as I thought it was him. It was a white woman and man, and they talked to my girlfriend in the kitchen. The woman came out of the kitchen and the feeling grew inside me even more. I rose up off the floor and approached her. She saw me but would not look directly at me; she thought I was a demon or something. I told her she had nothing to worry about, and she started talking, saying something in a low voice, still not looking at me. I just did not want to get mad at anyone.

11/30/99   5:51 a.m.   Pulling String from My Throat

I sat up; I had just finished pulling out of my throat and mouth what seems like miles of single strands of thread or cord. As I pulled it out with my hands, it felt like a giant rope. I could see it was colored black. I pulled on it for a long time, and I was not sure what I was really pulling out of my throat. A young woman pulled on it first, and I kept pulling it after that, with water and everything coming out.

This happened in the back alley of North West Street, where I lived. It all started when I walked into that alley and saw an apple tree with green apples. I started over to get one. As I walked, I saw blackberries on the vine, but I did not want those. They were so easy to get, but when I got to where the tree was supposed to be, it was not there, and I could not find it. I saw a lot of fruits and vegetables stored up in a storage area that had been a vacant lot, and as I walked a little further I saw this was a business, and a young black man operated it.

I started talking to him about his business. He sold a little bit of everything: he had a laundry, washed clothes, had a drug store, and sold medicine for children for only a dollar. I had left him to his customers and headed up the alley toward Pendleton Street when I saw kids who were just getting off a school bus. They walked up behind me, and that's when the young woman saw the single thread or cord coming out of my mouth and pulled on it. I continued to pull it out after that, and after a long while, it felt like a rope six or seven inches in diameter.

12/11/99   4:41 a.m.   A Pakistani Man Seems to Want to Attack a Man from India

I was getting in line to buy a drink, and there were many people trying to get something from this little carryout stand. As I got in line, just waiting for service and my turn, a very dark-skinned man, a man from Pakistan I think because of what happened later, said something out loud. While I stood there, the dark man said, "You know what should happen to some people," or something like that. I immediately got mad because he said an additional word, and it reminded me of the name black people were called. I said some words to him, since he was not that far from me—maybe ten or fifteen feet—but he paid no attention to me at all. He did get out of the line and went face-to-face with another man who looked like he was from India. They started to argue, and it looked like they were going to fight, but the man from India turned away from him. As he did, the Pakistani man walked up behind him. The Indian man wore a carpenter's belt with a hammer hanging from it, and I thought the Pakistani man would grab it and hit him from behind. He walked up behind him two times, as if he was going to grab the hammer out of his tool belt. He was clearly very angry, and it seemed as if he wanted to kill someone. The Indian man was a "carpenter look-alike."

Left and Right Hand Backside

12/23/99   3:16 a.m.   What Is a Thirty-Day Span of Time?

What was a thirty-day span of time? If it were solid, what would it look like? I got the chance to see the thirty-day time span kept. It was a new person, not one of the regulars, and when the new person showed me, I saw what they had. No one could say anything about it. It was not different, he was—a thirty-day span of time.

01/10/00   4:02 a.m.   I Had to Build a House and a Bridge

I was told to establish or build a house, and I had to build this house from or by way of a bridge or causeway. I had to build it in a certain manner with the instructions I was given, and I had to have it finished and furnished at a certain time. I did as I was told, but I also had questions about the house I had just finished. I also wanted to build myself a house on granddad's place, but it was off the road too far.

02/06/00   8:11 a.m.   Another Sun Man to Deal With

The voice said, "They have another sun man to deal with." Those were the words I heard.

8:36 a.m.   I Have Old Books to Learn the New Mechanics

I was given some very old books and was told they were for the new mechanics.

02/11/00   3:33 a.m.   I Looked Down with the One True God///
                          at Ezra in the Old Testament

I stood looking down from above, as a guest of the one God///, the Father///, as He/// first gave the gift of earthly wealth. I saw one woman with a ring in her hand, telling others that had had their backs turned to it about what had just happened. She told them about the mounds or hills of jewels, but when they turned to see it, nothing was there. The women looked up the hill, and I looked up the hill, but I did not see a mound of jewels. I did see a man picking one piece of fruit off a tree. He saw the woman, who was running toward him very fast. He ran too.

Now I was on the ground, and I sat by Ezra, and he had the fruit in his hands. But then I had it. He was old and feeble, and he cried over the days when the fruit was a ball of light and remembered how it glowed. It glowed no more; it was just fruit now. I took the fruit and, with my heart, I gave the fruit back to him once again, and he turned it and rubbed it to get it to glow one last time. I held him as he did that, and I could feel the life lift out of him. We faced south on Uncle Herbert's place. He passed on and his body crumbled to the ground. I held it but I could not stop it from happening.

I too cried. I now had the fruit, but it did not glow for me. The glow was as the light from heaven—given by the Father///, the light of the beginning. At this time, it was only him and me, and I think it was my mother who gave me the ball of light at the end.

02/20/00   1:17 a.m.   I Am Lifted Up, the Vibrations within Me
                          Revving Up

I felt the revving up of my body and real high vibrations, which lasted for a while. I was taken through the wall in a laying position, on my side, and then turned over on my stomach in a flying position and just let go. I raised my arms, and we went toward the river. He flew along behind me, talking, and then from his position, he reached around with both hands and touched each side of my head. He touched my ears and my eyes as if to shape or adjust them in some way, and then he talked to me. This was the first time a man had talked to me, and he pointed out below where General Powell's place was. He continued to talk about Powell for a while.

We flew side by side, and I did talk some but did not ask any questions about where we were going. The high vibration was a spinning motion, yet I did not feel like I was spinning, but I felt as I did when going through the wall. I was spinning at such a high rate that it did not seem like it.

03/15/00   12:30 a.m.   I'm Taken, Stood on My Head Completely Upside Down

I was lying in bed and then lifted and taken. I was turned on my head, like times before, with my face to the floor and my feet up in the air. This time it was not at an angle as it was before. Then I was moved to a laying position, and I began to turn like a drill bit. I was taken through a concrete floor very slowly. It was made with steel rebar, and I was seeing all of it as I went through.

I lay on the ground, and then I felt a jolt like an electric shock run through me. I knew this time it was me having to put forth direct effort. It was as if the shock came from me. I was taken again, going through all the same things: the wall, floor, steel rebar, concrete, and pipes in the walls. My body was spinning with my head being the front tip of the drill bit, but I went through everything this time.

The difference was, when I got to the steel reinforcement bars and the six—to ten-inch diameter pipe, my spinning body slowed down like a drill bit, but it picked up speed as I went through them. A couple of times, when I went through the concrete floor, it was wet, and the floor looked like I had wrecked the house with a wrecking ball. My whole body was turning like a high-speed diamond drill bit, and through all of this, I was held and guided. I got through seams and corners and all the hardest parts of a building, and I ended up at North West Street, where the water and plaster were all over the floor.

03/28/00   2:44 a.m.   Right Hand Backside

04/08/00   7:10 a.m.   Joe Gibbs, Coach of the Washington
                         Football Team

I was on a professional football team in Washington DC where Joe Gibbs was the coach and Brian Mitchell returned kick-offs. We were waiting for the football to come down out of the air, and I was on the line to block for Brian as he got it. I started to block, and that fast, Brian was passing me, going into the open field. I saw him go fifty yards before they stopped him. Coach Gibbs had a boy who was eight to ten years old run onto the field when the play was over to get the football and replace it with a another one. It seemed as if the coach did not want anyone to put their hands on the footballs we used for kickoffs.

Then I was on another team, and Don, a friend was in charge. He had me looking for hubcaps on vehicles that would be turned in for replacements—two teams, two coaches.

04/10/00   6:23 a.m.   Left Hand Backside

Book XVI

05/13/00   3:54 a.m.   Moved from Corner to Corner

I was in bed when a woman I knew got in bed with me and started to have fun all on her own. When I started to join in and pay attention to her, she faded; it happened all the time. I had thought she had come back, when I was lifted out of bed, and a hand behind my head pulled my face along the walls of my apartment. This had all happened before, in December of 1992, but this time I was pulled around the base of the wall until I got to the door, and then I was pulled up and over top of the door and down the other side. I was moved the whole length of the wall in the living room face up against the wall at the base, almost on the floor, but no part of my body ever touched the floor.

I silently asked "to understand what I was being shown, taught, or prepared for." Back at my bedroom, I was moved again along the wall to the front door. I was moved up and around that door, and I woke up sitting on the side of my bed with a lamp fixture in my left hand, trying to find the little lamp on the dresser with my right hand. Then I woke up again and really woke up.

This vision is similar to the 1992 vision, except I am now at the base of the wall, taking in the root of the things I need to know for the outside. This, in some fashion, will happen again, but I will be taken outside into the world, and the lamp fixture in my left hand is my source. My looking for the other lamp with my right hand is my knowledge being used in the world—first light was brought to me, and then I shared it with the world.

05/23/00   6:25 a.m.   Left Hand Backside

05/27/00   10:07 a.m.   Shown the Puzzle of Life

I was in bed looking at the television. A thunderstorm started, and it was raining and there was lightning, and the wind had started to blow, but I could not hear a thing. I saw it all but heard nothing for some reason. I had heard the television but not even that now. I was just wondered what was happening. The storm seemed so powerful, and yet I heard nothing. The wind was blowing with gale-force winds and the lighting seemed bad and very close.

I continued to look at the television, and in the middle of a cartoon-type program, I began to feel like I was going to be taken. I had the feeling of vibrations. As I felt the vibrations, I was in a state of being able to be trained. I started to see everything on the television as if it were a puzzle. I could see all the pieces and how they fit. Each puzzle part represented people, buildings, cars, plants, and animals. It was a story, but it showed everything outlined in a puzzle that was all put together. As the program went on from scene to scene and place to place, it all continued to be in puzzle form but was completely together and everything fit.

05/31/00   10:32 a.m.   Left Hand Backside

This was a new combination control and watch assembly with rings. The watch and rings were all one piece, connected in the palm area down to the wrist, where it made a three-quarter circle around the wrist and clamped soundlessly in place.

06/01/00   10:30 a.m.   Left Hand & Right Hand

06/02/00   4:37 a.m.   I Wrote a Formula on a Blackboard

I was trying not to make a mistake with the information I had. We traveled across Parker Gray High School's field to a place where we placed medical prescriptions of some kind on top of a book. I started to write them on the blackboard, 2CA7 "*2*"A, but I was not sure of the last character, and I needed to be exact. I placed the formula on the book for a guy with me, and I did not feel sure of it. It could have been 4AC2 "*2*", I looked at all the other medical formulas, and they were all in order. This one had to be right too.

Right Hand Backside and Forearm

06/04/00   4:23 a.m.   What is the Hebrew Sign for a Baby

I woke up, and as I lifted my head to get up, I heard these words, "What is the sign for Hebrew baby?" I understood the question, but why would I be asked that? And then I really woke up.

Left Forearm

11:38 a.m.   Right Hand Backside

07/03/00   8:35 a.m.   Left Hand Backside

07/09/00   4:09 a.m.   The One Called Death Pointed at Me

I was learning about a robber who was also a thief and most of all a murderer. He killed them and possessed them through their spirits. I heard about him, or whatever he was, and I began to feel very scared—so much so that I would not even go outside of my place. One day, I was running away, and I started thinking about myself as I ran. I was not that good of a person anyway, and that was when I found myself in the very spot I feared the most. I was out in a large open area, fearing everything that moved, and it happened just as I was told it would. As I stood, too scared to move, I saw off in the distance the very creature I feared the most. It came on horseback straight at me, but it veered off a little, because behind him were lots of others after him. He saw me and turned his head in my direction just long enough to say something and point up the road. He said, "Way up the road is a box full of body parts. That's where you will go."

I was scared, and I knew something must have happened up there. The next thing I knew, I saw what looked like a cannon blast hit a metal container and rock the whole thing while men on guard stood by. They were guarding with guns, but they withdrew into themselves when they saw it, and I wondered what soul, too horrible know or see, had done this.

I did not know how long I was there, but something happened to me, and I was taken up from that place and became new. I then became physical and spirit, seen and unseen. I flew with the wind, looking around everywhere, getting those I wanted. This same place had many people who had lost their spirit and had become as the living dead, and I had come for one of them. I flew around just above her head, and I told her I had come for her. She warned me about the ones inside and said that they would be mad and would attack me if I tried. I told her to let me worry about that—I had come for her, and I would have her body and soul. I had become the one I feared most.

07/11/00   5:51 a.m.   Watching Myself Sitting in a Chair with
                         Many Arms and Legs (Buddhism)

I was looking at myself sitting in a chair and was trying to figure out what I was really looking at. I saw my body with arms, legs, and a head, all sticking out of one body at every angle. I continued to watch.

I See a Tibetan Monk Who Looks like the Dalai Lama

I was driving a four-wheel-drive vehicle, and I turned off into what I thought was a large parking area, but it was filled with sand, beautiful colored sand—mounds of it. On my right, I saw a monk. I believe it was a Tibetan monk, and from the little I saw of him from the back, I believe it was the Dalai Lama himself. I did not see a face, but I did see the orange cloak. I wanted to stop and get closer, but it would not have been right to do that or bother him. I slowly turned my vehicle around and came out of the parking area off the sand. The parking area had a small shopping center around it also.

07/18/00   11:28 p.m.   I Could Only Say "Father///, Take Me, Do What You/// Will"

I knelt down to pray, but I found that this time I could only say, "Father///, take me; do what you will with me." I got into bed and lay on my left side. I began to feel physically and spiritually bad, and as I went off to sleep, it seemed as if I was losing life. I felt as if I might die or have a heart attack. As I turned over on my right side, I felt the same but a bit relieved, and I drifted off to sleep.

I first felt that vibrating feeling and then felt being lifted, going somewhere. I saw myself; I saw hands inside my head, and my head felt and sounded as if it had a bad small motor on the left side of it. I almost wanted to be scared, but I knew to be quiet and still and just let it happen. What I heard was a sound like a broken fan blade inside a water pump for a car, but then it got better. A hand moved across my head to different points as if to adjust them one at a time until it reached just above my left ear area. The sound smoothed out all over once that was done. Then it traced from there down, and I felt it from the inside of my neck to my throat and mouth area. (There was so much more to this.)

I was taken up and carried to an open area where there was a tree. I was being held, and something happened to me there. I felt a presence like Jesus/// in me. We were the same spirit, and I was facing the tree. Hands were carrying me, and they felt like male hands until this point.

Then I was on my own feet as I stood with kids, and they came all around me. I talked to them, and I knelt down and held them. I went to a couple of places very fast, taken by the hand of the one with me a very long way at great speed, greater than any other time. I would seem to be going a certain speed and then change to a higher speed, and the wind at dusk before dark was all I saw as I was carried from behind. I began to feel the hands that I had felt many times before, but this time they were electrified, and it was like holding an exposed electric cord with volts just high enough to withstand. This lasted the entire flight until we arrived at a place where I was put down. I met kids again who talked to me and helped me. I was shown the door of a house of a religious denomination, and he had just sent kids out of his house. I went to his door, and as I knocked, he came out of the door right passed me and gave me no attention at all. As he walked by I asked him to help me, but he seemed offended that I had asked. (See vision in 1984.)

07/21/00   5:40 a.m.   Interviewing For a Job

I interviewed for a job, and I got it. I was told when to come back and start. I left the manager's office and went to his office assistant to get more information. I asked her what things I needed to know for the job and asked what could I study to do a good job. She was going to write down two things for me but had trouble removing the cover on her ballpoint pen. It was new, and I took it off for her. I told her I planned to attend school, taking classes in the evening and on weekends to improve myself to get ready for the job.

I interviewed for a job in September 1992. I found I was able to foretell the future thirty days out exactly; it will happen again in 2012, but there is more. This is about writing books, and the date is 2011, around May to July. But this vision will start full force in 2012, using the Mayan eleven-year and twenty-year calendars. It could be a larger job than I am writing about.

07/22/00   2:48 a.m.   Lamps in All the Corners

I was laying in my bed when I started to feel vibrations all over me. I was lifted up with my feet above my head. My head and hands were down where my feet usually were. I was carried around my bedroom three times, counterclockwise, and then lifted into an upright position. I was carried up through the floors of the apartments above me and positioned in the corners of each apartment, one above the other. As I was being lifted up in the corner of my bedroom, I saw a lamp on the dresser in the opposite corner. As I was lifted up through each floor in the very same corner of the apartments, I saw a very beautiful rustic lamp set up.

Then I was brought back to my bedroom, and I could hear myself snoring a bit. When I was first taken around the room counterclockwise, I thought I was going to knock everything off the dresser on to the floor, but nothing was touched.

07/31/00   6:01 a.m.   Twinkling Stars, a Mother and Children

I was lying down in my bedroom. Mama had just finished talking to me about something, and I was not yet asleep when I saw something. When I lifted my head to get a better look, I saw something I had never seen before. It was like a group of colored lightning bugs. Except these were small twinkling stars of different colors that moved as they pleased, all making the same movement at the same time. There was one large star, and to me, it was like the mother and the small ones were her children. They were all around her, twinkling as they moved across my room, left to right, to the door and out. They did this three times. I watched her take her children, twinkling different colors all the time, and stop in midair three times. Then she left with them.

Later, in my vision as I slept, I saw all this again, but only once this time—the same beautiful little stars, a mother and children, and so many different colors like a rainbow. And as they left, I said thank-you, but maybe I should have just been quiet.

It was morning, and Mama was talking about cantaloupe and some big prize for the size of one we bought in Culpepper, Virginia, which was six or seven pounds.

08/02/00   1:32 a.m.   I Must Be Fishing for Fisherman

I was fishing on the river, and I found I had thrown my line across the other fisherman to my left. I would tangle their lines if I pulled mine in. It was all just a vision, but one day I did grab my gear and go fishing, and I remembered the vision and moved down river, away from any other fisherman. I cast my line out and did not see where it went. It was the longest cast I had ever made—it seemed like a mile. When I started to pull it back in, I had crossed every fisherman on the river anyway. I had done it again, and this time it was not a vision. I decided to pull it in; I would try to yank it up and over their lines. I yanked it, and it landed on a fisherman, sinker and all. I was far enough away from them that they could not see me. I did not know what else to do. I made the cast. I looked up in the air, and it went over everything thing else on the water. Fishing—it seemed as if the only thing I was fishing for was fishermen.

08/03/00   1:32 a.m.   Wish Upon a Star

I went to sleep and saw myself looking out of a window and remembered a song I used to hear in my head when I was a boy: "When you wish upon a star, makes no difference who you are, anything your heart desires, will come to you."

I was about eleven or twelve years old and my favorite song was "When You Wish upon a Star" because all I thought about was "what if." I did not have any ideas of being anything; I just looked out the window at the stars.

08/05/00   5:16 a.m.   I Saw the Man Who Looked like Me

I saw the man who looked like me, and it was Jesus, coming out of a door. Before this, my girlfriend had prepared a place for me on the floor by my bed, and I lay on her right side down there. I lay beside her, but I was on an air mattress on the floor, and I did not like it. She asked if I wanted to change, and I said yes, and then I lay on her right still but on a pallet of cloth of some type.

I started to feel vibrations, and I was left that way for a while. I saw Jesus walking out of a place just before I heard my name called. I heard a woman over the intercom call my name, "Ed," and I answered very low, like her page. I answered a second and third time in the same low voice, and that was when I felt the vibrations come over me. I saw what I thought was an animation—like a cartoon—happening, and Jesus walked out of a furniture store. I saw the furniture change to African Egyptian furniture with signs and symbols on the walls.

It all started to backup and to back out from the earth, and my view of everything was moving up and away from the earth very fast. I first saw the continent of Africa as it backed out and moved, and then I saw North America and the West Coast area. It backed out more, and I saw our planet, our solar system, and many stars. I saw planetary systems, one after the other, all in a line with darkness surrounding or separating them.

Next, I found myself back in the store with furniture and people, but all of this seemed as one thing. The way I was shown or led was by the one in front of me, walking before me.

5:16 a.m.   Left Hand Backside

9:50 a.m.   Women Sit on Two Sides in This Large Professional Facility

I was in a large professional facility with just women, and they sat on two sides of the floor. On one side, women sat who wore feminine pads and the insertion type devices for **feminine** hygiene. On the other side of the floor, women were not allowed to use the insertion devices, maxi pads, or anything like that for some reason. I did not know if there was a taboo or religious problem with women taking care of themselves as they needed to.

11:01 a.m.   My Father and I Both Sit in the Same Seat

I was standing, talking, when my father came up behind me and grabbed my hands and held them so I could not move them. I began to feel my strength, but I remained still and he continued to hold them. I sat down in a chair, and my father sat behind me. It was as if we were two people acting as one, but each with his own space, as I sat forward of him.

08/12/00   6:39 a.m.   Sheriff in Midwest Town Selling Guns

I was working with a federal taskforce on illegal gun sales, and we were tracking a group that bought guns generally from protected sources or law enforcement sources. We had been tracking this bunch for a while, and we tracked them to a small Midwest town where we found out the sheriff was involved. The sheriff was the source of the movement of guns this time, but our problem was that this group never left witnesses to testify.

We found out quickly how things were done in this small town. We found the family of the sheriff and talked to them. They knew about what was going on. They did not realize how wrong it was. We were faced with a time problem; we did not want anyone else to end up dead. We had to question the family and tell them the end result of every deal done by this group in the past. They came clean, because they did not want the sheriff to end up dead.

I was looking at a boy who had just been shot in the arm. He was the grandson of the sheriff, and we knew the sheriff would be next. We thought that in fifteen minutes to an hour it would be over for this family, one way or the other. If I did not make it in time, I would end up praying, asking the Father/// to hold the life force in the sheriff until I could get him medical treatment.

08/19/00   2:53 a.m.   I Meet with Women Who Have Many Problems

I was in a room, waiting for the people coming in. They all seem to be women. I had them sit in chairs in a circle around the room as I prepared to start the meeting. I closed my eyes, turned around in my chair, and called out a name, and that person came up to talk to me. When we were finished talking she had had her problem taken care of, and she left. They all came in and sat down. They did not talk to anyone or tell anyone anything about themselves while they were there.

I called up two people at one time. The first one I talked to and sent home; to the second one I said, "I want to put my arms around you." As I did, I felt a pointed bone on her right side sticking out a little. It was a growth; That's when she told me her problem. As she did, I pushed the bone back in its place. It was as one naturally should be. She felt back there and started to declare her feelings. I told her to sit in a chair for a while, and we continued to talk. I did not think she could have sat down before at all because of the bone sticking out.

I then called on Ms. Bryant. I saw the lady as she walked up, and it was someone I knew. I told her, "I didn't know your name was Bryant," as she moved back and forth. There was a small girl with her, and it was the child I wanted to see and talk to, not her. I reached for the child, but after seeing her mother, I knew I might have to do something for her too. I could see the mother's problem as she spit up something from her mouth on the floor. She did not look good at all, but it might have been her own doing. It might have been the reason I was called to help the child and not her.

8:28 a.m.   A Picture of a Giant Cross Turned Sideways

I saw a large picture in my vision as I stood under a giant cross pulled sideways. Long string-type strands were hanging down from it. It was an outdoor picture, like a watercolor painting but black and white, as if the painter forgot to color it. The cross was full of everything, all kinds of things but nothing you could talk about, and the strings were different sizes and on every part of the cross.

It seems as if the cross is weighted down, and the strings, being different sizes, represent people, organizations, religious ideologies that have added to the original meaning of the cross and what it stood for. The cross is a physical and spiritual weight that each of us must take on with our heads high, knowing the outcome. Whatever our faith, it must have a true root that our present day ideology sprang from. Since early times, there have been many changes and revisions to it. The point is, it has been changed and revised too much; the strings are how we have varied from the original meaning to make it fit our needs and to go so far as to use it to cause death in some kind of holy or spiritual war voiced by some.

08/25/00   6:00 a.m.   Left Hand Backside

8:38 a.m.   Charlie Sheen and I Worked for the Government

I was on Interstate 295, headed into Washington DC with Charlie. We were just called into the office, and it was a good bet that one of us had a chance at the White House protection detail with the President. I had been waiting for a chance at that for a long time, actually both Charlie and I had.

We ran into a problem on 295, an auto accident bad enough that one of us had to stay until local police arrived. I decided it would be me, and that just about put me out of any chance of getting that position; if Charlie went in alone, he had it.

Much later, we were talking again, out near 295, and this time it was Charlie, Clint Eastwood, and me remembering old times. As we stood there, a patrol officer bought Clint a map of the area—495, 295, and 95—so he could figure out something. He had it on his mind to reduce the speed limit to 35 mph, crawling speed just before the beltway. His wife was on the beltway driving, and he wanted me to look out for her because he did not know the area well enough to instruct her.

Book XVII

09/03/00   6:43 a.m.   So Many People Coming to See Me

I was sitting on a stump in empty lot on Payne Street near Queen Street in the 1300 block. I was sitting there on the stump, looking at everything that was happening around me. I felt I must have been very old with all white hair. People stared at me.

So many people were all over this place, and I saw one young white boy with his mother and father. As the boy looked at me, I reached out to him. I said, "Come here, young man." He stared back at me until his mother pushed him toward me. He looked to be five or six years old, and as we talked, I asked him a couple of questions as his parents looked on. I put out my hand to shake his and he just looked at me. I said, "Don't be afraid," and he put his hand out too and began to talk. He then walked with his parents from right front to a rear area of some kind on the right side. So many people are in line; I sat on the stump, looking at them as they walked up.

09/10/00   1:35 a.m.   A Special Path to Walk

I was in bed, and I got that feeling of vibrations. I was lifted up and taken for a certain time along a concrete path with high walls on both sides. My feet and hands touched the sides of the walls. Then we went through a concrete barrier in front of us that led into a cinderblock pathway with high walls on both sides. We continued to travel along this path for a certain time. It was very long too, and at the end, a cinderblock barrier was in front of us, just like the concrete barrier.

We traveled at medium speed the whole time, and hands were carrying me under my arms. I knew this is not a woman. I could not see anyone, but I knew or felt that this was all right.

I was taken through the cinderblock barrier into the beautiful blue night. It was a medium-blue haze, and everything could be seen. Where I was, was a large body of dark blue mixed air and water; it was a mixture for birth and rebirth, and you could breathe it as easy as air itself. The whole time the one stood with me who carried me. As I stood in the watery mix, breathing it, I looked at the one with me, seeing him and not seeing him; I saw and yet I did not see, and there was no impression left of him. This lasted a long time, and my thoughts were on the different areas that I had come through. They all seemed to have been in a straight line, but no thought at all was on what was after all this.

Then I was taken to where there were many people—it seemed mostly women. This all happened twice. I was taken on the path twice and met the people twice, and then I was told something in my left ear. I was told it in two parts, or I was told the same thing a second time.

I was turned loose, and I said, "Thank you, God///," and I went through all the people again, but this time it was different. This time, they were pushing and pulling on me and shaking my hand, and some were doing everything they could think as I walked past, but I did not stop. I walked away from where all these people were, but two women still held onto me, saying to stay. I raised my hands toward the sky, and said that I must go—I could not stay.

I was taken up, going back on the same path again: the blue, long area of birth fluid you could breathe, the cinderblock path with high walls, the concrete path with its high walls, and then to my bed.

First, my bed is my workplace, and the trip I must make is a type of trip we all must make. Some trips are different from others. The barriers are levels of understanding, at first a little difficult, then the porous cinderblock is where it gets a little easier, and then the living waters. This all may take many lifetimes, and that may be at odds with some beliefs, but at some point you find out you have to actually make the trip by yourself, meaning what you actually understand and stand on will be your judge. I will spiritually and physically walk this path during this lifetime, it is structured on all sides, and I walk it alone physically.

09/19/00   4:50 a.m.   Right Hand Backside

10:42 a.m.   OneOther Shows Me What He Is

I was on the way to a friend's house, following her, and it turned out that it was not who I thought it was. I followed her into the house anyway, and she led me to her bedroom. On the way, I saw a seven-foot shelving unit full of dishes that did not look right. The shelving unit was leaning out, away from the wall over the hallway, as if the dishes were going to fall off. I tried to push some of them back a little. We entered the bedroom and there sat a woman and a child on the bed. They got up and left right away. She told me to close the blinds and go up the hall to the other room with the two chandeliers in it to get something.

I passed the shelving again, and it was leaning over even more—almost touching the opposite wall, but the dishes still did not fall off. It seemed funny to me how the things on the shelf did not fall off; I even had to bend over to pass under it to get to the other room. I went into the room and saw an old-style chandelier, with the wax candles lit, hanging in the center of the room. I saw another chandelier just like it, but it was hanging in the air about four feet from the ceiling, upside down, and it was hanging by nothing at all. There was no support and the candles were still burning as if it was in the upright position. It seemed like most everything up in the ceiling area was just hanging there. The chandelier was upside down, yet it was still on, without anything supporting it.

As I walked into the room, right away I felt an electrical energy charge go all through me. I was then flipped upside down and held by one leg, my head down and legs up. I could see I was held by something I could not describe. Then I was put down on a bed. I tried to move, but I could not. What held me was making gestures with its body, but I could not understand what it was trying to say. Then I began to understand it a little, and I thought it was trying to say, "I did sit-ups, two or three of them." That's what I got. Then it came to me and it was made clear to me, "not sit-up, but raised-up." With a hand, it went from a low position to a high one, and with the hand stretched out, I knew it meant a child, small now but growing. I knew he meant it was me who was raised up, from a child until now. Then what I could not describe became a man, a white-colored spirit form of a man, and he began to talk to me in English. He said, "I have been with you since you were born; I took care of you always." We talked on. I never saw the women again that I was with earlier, and none of this was or is a surprise to me because all along OneOther was and is always with me.

09/22/00   3:28 a.m.   Standing on the Path Waiting to Be Called On

We were given a place in time until we were called on for services. We had a few pairs of shoes, and one pair would be called on. This same procedure had happened a few times in our past, and it had happened again. The lady and I stood waiting on the path.

09/30/00   5:16 a.m.   Left hand backside

10/01/00   7:10 a.m.   The True Meaning of a Dream

I was in a crowded place, sitting in a booth. I heard a friend I knew very well being told what her dream meant. As she talked to them, she explained the dream to them, and a number of people around her started to tell her what it meant all at once. They were all saying different things. Part of the dream was "there is a man standing between my friend, a female, and her boyfriend." Actually, it was as simple as could be, and the true answer was "do not make any serious decisions about your boyfriend now, because very soon there will be another man in your life, and you will put him between you your boyfriend." A man was coming and she would want him more than the one she had now, so no rash decisions. As I sat there, they just kept giving her all kinds of ideas about what that dream meant. Another guy sat down where my friend and I were, and he began to tell my friend, a female, that she had won some awards and he had them with him. He looked at me and said, "You've won some too, seven or eight of them, and he handed me a book and said the awards were in it. I opened the book, and it looked like a check was in with the awards. I turned away and started to talk to my friend again.

The true meaning of a dream is at least three-fold when trying to understand it. First, it is like being opposite, like inside out. The second part is the fact that you can change it depending on what type of dream or vision it is. And third, if it is a vision that seems to be very important or destructive, you only have a certain time to try to change it. Some visions will never change, the outcome will remain the same because we fail to change. It is wonderful to be shown problems and trouble in advance, but if you stay on the same path, nothing will change.

8:10 a.m.   My Garden Plot

I was sitting at the table, outlining my garden, drawing where everything would be placed in it. That was when I noticed that my garden looked exactly like the pyramid area in Egypt—with the pyramids and everything. I had people traveling the highway around all the structures, but it was my garden plot.

10/15/00   7:10 a.m.   Crossing the Land Bridge to the Doctor Who is Six or Seven Years Old

I was in a yard surrounded by kids, except these kids held their own—age was not a hindrance. We had an almost-grown lion running around in the yard with everyone else, leaving its eliminations everywhere. I called the lion to come. He looked and came. I walked him around to the kitchen. Our doctor was in the kitchen area; she was our doctor and part leader—she was only six years old. She told me we had to get medicine from another place so we could cure the lion. I decided to go and get the medicine as fast as I could. I walked a very long way, until I came to the great water that I crossed by a land bridge. The waters held both salt and fresh water fish of all kinds at the surface and just below. I traveled onto where she said the doctor was. When I got there, there were many people in line, waiting for potions of all kinds. The doctor was about the same as our doctor, six or seven years old, and she was able to heal many types of animals. There were younger kids here, no more than two or three years old. One group of three had come together: one of them was four or five years old, and the other two were no more than two or three years old. I saw no grown people, except for myself; all were the size of children. She had so many waiting in line that I decided to take a walk back toward the land bridge to see the fish again. As I returned to the doctors' place, I heard someone say to the three kids I saw earlier as they were heading away, "Don't fall in." They played like kids and acted as if they might but they didn't. So many people were waiting for help.

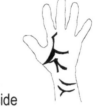

11/09/00   7:01 a.m.   Right Hand Backside

11/26/00   5:45 a.m.   Right Forearm

12/20/00   5:50 a.m.   Do I Want to Finish or Win

I had been trying to decide if I wanted to finish or wanted to win, and it had something to do with Tracy, who was a friend, and just living my life. I did not really know the answer. I saw some young people playing and just thought that would be my answer. The young people each had rings on their fingers, one each, that looked like Olympic competition rings, and they gave off a type of light. It reminded me of the Olympic torch flame that burns all the time. The rings the kids had gave off a glow and a light, as if they had a flame too. As I got closer, I saw the colors in the rings were a bluish, greenish, and red, and from its surface, it looked like water and light mixed together.

I was back in my room, thinking about the rings the young people had on and if I wanted to win or finish. I decided again that I did not want to win or finish; I wanted to live and work hard, and the end result would determine itself. Every day I wanted to do the best I could, and if in the end, I had finished or won, what would I have finished and what I would have won the Father/// would have determined.

Just as the kids were playing, I want to just play the game. The outcome, it is what I learned from Meg, a friend who actually showed me how to play the game.

Author Biography

Edmond L. Campbell was born in Warrenton, Virginia, in 1947, and moved to the Alexandria/Fairfax area early in his childhood. Everything Edmond knows and understands about his extended history came from his spiritual experiences that have happened since childhood.

"I remember my first vision; I was five years old, and it was about my mother dying." The unusual part of that vision was that the mother who loved and raised Edmond was not the mother who was dying in his dream. It would be a year later that Edmond would find out that he was adopted. That experience was the start of Edmond's visionary experience—and the start of this book, which has been thirty years in the making.

Edmond, formally Director with United Way Worldwide, is now retired and lives with his family in Alexandria, Virginia.